DISCI-PLESHIP PROJECT

LUCAS LEYS
DAVID NOBOA

DISCI-PLESHIP PROJECT

LUCAS LEYS
DAVID NOBOA

e625.com

DISCIPLESHIP PROJECT—CHILDREN'S MINISTRY
e625 - 2023
Dallas, Texas
e625 ©2023 by **Lucas Leys and David Noboa**

All Bible verses are from the New International Version (NIV) unless otherwise specified.

Translated by: Josiah Brown

Interior Design and Cover: JuanShimabukuroDesign

ISBN: 978-1-954149-51-9

PRINTED IN THE UNITED STATES

CONTENTS

INTRO

Success is only a consequence of having developed discipline with perseverance.

Lucas Leys, *Stamina*

In the Bible we find the story of when Jesus, after his resurrection, had an encounter with two of his disciples while they were walking towards Emmaus, a city located 10 kilometers from Jerusalem. As we read in this story from Luke chapter 24, those who claimed to be his followers did not know, at that moment, who he was. Doesn't that statement intrigue you? How is it that those who recognized themselves as his followers could not recognize him? The answers can be many... Some illustrate Jesus hidden behind a cloak, others say that his glorified image was different from his human form previous to the crucifixion, or perhaps he had the ability to confuse people's eyes so that they did not recognize him. The truth is that they did not know who he was until the moment he broke the bread and only then could they recognize him.

Whatever the explanation, the story highlights a powerful truth: It is not enough to know who Jesus is. Jesus can walk with you without you being able to recognize him, and suddenly, poof! a great revelation comes into your life that makes you see clearly that Jesus has been walking and talking with you the whole time.

THAT IS THE TASK OF THE DISCIPLERS: WALK WITH SOMEONE SO THEY CAN CLEARLY SEE JESUS

That is the task of disciplers: walk with someone so that they can clearly see Jesus; accompanying another who still cannot recognize him in certain aspects of their life. And that is the challenge of biblical discipleship: traveling with another person until they can recognize the Messiah, their inner blindfolds drop, and they experience the presence of God through the risen Christ.

WHAT DISCIPLESHIP IS NOT:

On many occasions, the clearest way to define something is to list what it is not, and here is a list of what biblical discipleship is not:

- **IT IS NOT A BIBLE CLASS.** Usually, these two expressions get confused with each other since they often go hand in hand, but they are not the same. Teaching the Bible is an indispensable part of discipleship and that is why this book contains lessons to teach. However, this book includes the word *project* because just teaching a Bible class is not the whole of discipleship.

- **IT IS NOT A MEMBERSHIP PROGRAM.** In some churches it is believed that discipleship is an initiation program for new believers, but again, we want new believers to start being disciples of Jesus and it is great that there is a good program for those who are taking their first steps in faith. But discipleship does not end with baptism or with the completion of a course. It is not about attending a series of workshops. Although this can help a lot in the discipleship process, you will see that biblical knowledge and other types of learning do not necessarily result in greater spiritual maturity.

- **IT IS NOT A DOCTRINAL REFLECTION.** Discipleship is not limited to intellectual matters. Rather, it is a process of integral character development that involves, in addition to the brain, the spirit, emotions, will, and conduct. Theology classes could make us fall into the delusion that by learning certain doctrines, we will be good disciples. The doctrines, of course, are fundamental and there is doctrinal teaching in true biblical discipleship, but those doctrines must be put into action to have an effect. Knowing theology and doctrine does not make you a good disciple if it does not lead to a tangible practice. Consider, for example, the Pharisees, whom Jesus was confronting. They had a lot of knowledge, and they handled theology and doctrine perfectly, but their hearts were far from God.

- **IT IS NOT A LITURGY.** Although it is true that discipleship has a lot to do with acquiring good habits and spiritual disciplines, these things should not become cold repetitions or rigid religious behavior. Each discipline acquired, each moment of collective worship, each act of community participation, prayer, and fasting, are tools for our hearts to be conquered by the heart of Jesus and not only for us to "do" what is right in the eyes of others.

One can know a lot about God and be far from him, and because of this, genuine discipleship is more like being a mirror of Christ than simply teaching about him.

The point is not to "show" who is more like Jesus but to be clear that the more I focus on willingly reflecting Christ, the better discipler I will be.

So, what is biblical discipleship? Putting together just one sentence that includes all that genuine discipleship means can be very daring. . . but we can try:

CHRISTIAN DISCIPLESHIP IS A PROCESS OF ACCOMPANIMENT IN WHICH, THROUGH A PERSONAL RELATIONSHIP, SOMEONE IS ABLE TO FACILITATE IN THE DISCIPLE THE VIRTUES OF THE CHARACTER OF JESUS.

THINK OF THESE TWO WORDS:

- **PROCESS:** Discipleship is a progressive and patient process. It has to do with accompanying a person from one place to another, just as it happened with the travelers in Emmaus. As they walked, Jesus reminded them of things they had already heard and told them things they did not yet know. And they lived the "process" of that walk with such intensity that when they finally realized it was their Master, they remembered that their hearts burned while he spoke to them.

- **RELATIONSHIP:** Discipleship does not happen without accompaniment. Walking together with someone means "being there" for that person. It's not just about giving lessons or classes, and it needs to be more than just a weekly meeting. Discipleship goes beyond being together for church services or scheduled meetings. The best disciplers share other moments of life with their apprentices and that is why the lessons in this book will challenge you to move from the lesson into community. That's how Jesus did it. And that is how we will do it.

THE MORE I FOCUS ON VOLUNTARILY REFLECTING CHRIST, THE BETTER DISCIPLER I WILL BE

The twelve disciples were not the only followers of Jesus, but they were the most intimate. Throughout the time that our Messiah walked among human beings, many were close to him and that is still true today. Do you remember the crowd eating freely of the loaves and fishes?

There may be many followers of Jesus, but not all who claim to follow him are truly his disciples.

The Bible says that the Word became flesh and dwelt among us. He lived with men proclaiming that the kingdom of heaven had drawn near. He died. He rose again. And just before leaving to return to the throne prepared for him, he left a great task: *Go and make disciples, teach them to observe all the things that I have told you.* Then it is said that around 500 people witnessed the ascension of the Savior (1 Corinthians 15:6).

The great task of making disciples of all nations is being carried out with various nuances, and in initiating this project in our churches, the imperative question to answer is: How can we make better disciples of Jesus?

As you go through this book, you will be given 10 crucial premises about the different aspects that biblical discipleship represents. Beyond the transmission of knowledge, these premises are intended to help you in the transmission of a CUL-TURE. That is what Christ came to establish: the culture of the kingdom of heaven, the precise interpretation of what the Father had said since ancient times, the social exercise of a people, which we now call family, and the characteristics that this family must have. As you can see, these are valuable things that we cannot forget.

Jesus announced that he had come to fulfill the law and not to abolish it, but he did not teach his disciples a series of steps to be better believers. He lived a lifestyle of faith with them. Jesus was with his disciples even in the most difficult moments, but he did not gather them together to give them a talk on obedience. He obeyed the Father in everything, and thus taught them to do the same.

> *This is the covenant I will make with them after that time, says the Lord. I will put my laws in their hearts, and I will write them on their minds.*
>
> (Hebrews 10:16)

PRIOR TRAINING FOR DISCIPLERS

Your church and ministry can do transformational discipleship and this preliminary training is intended to:

- Break any incorrect paradigm that exists around biblical discipleship in the understanding of your team members.

- Excite and encourage your volunteers with the challenging and wonderful project of making your participants more like Jesus.

- Optimize the growth process by establishing clear results for your ministry.

- Expand the vision of all those involved, recovering the sense of community of the first century church.

ESSENTIAL PRINCIPLES OF BIBLICAL DISCIPLESHIP

WE ARE THE CHURCH

The greatest gift a church can receive is to have a group of families who take their responsibilities with such Christian seriousness that they are willing to completely alter their lifestyle to raise up disciples for Jesus Christ.

Abraham Kuyper

For a long time, we got so used to having meetings in a temple as part of the natural exercise of the church that this inertia produced in us a forgetfulness. We forgot we must be and make disciples, and not just attend meetings. In a biblical sense, the church is not a place to go, but a family to belong to, and if we fail to see it in this way, we will end up stunting our personal growth and that of the church.

The way we speak exhibits how we think and, consequently, how we act. Look at this conversation.

—What church do you go to?

—I attend Central Church.

—But... are you one of those who serve?

— I only attend, I am not in any ministry.

THE CHURCH IS NOT A PLACE TO GO, BUT A FAMILY TO BELONG TO.

Surely you heard something similar. But the truth is that "attending" an ecclesial community is practically impossible from God's perspective. Think of your family.

Do you attend your family weekly or are you part of it? Being part of the church and congregating is not the same as attending.

A biblical answer to the above question would be:

—I do not attend a church; I *am* the church of Christ.

Another very common comment is the following:

—I didn't go to church this week.

And their leader replies: —Well, you shouldn't miss it because remember we shouldn't stop congregating.

Nobody has bad intentions when saying these things but doing so can push the new generations to lead a double life. What exactly is congregate? Obviously, the word means to come together but in a biblical sense it means to be linked. Share a feeling, a belief, and a practical coexistence.

SAYING "WE ARE THE CHURCH" LETS US KNOW THAT WE ARE PART OF THE CHURCH AND WE WILL NEVER STOP BEING SO.

We must avoid having on one side of life: church meetings in which everyone is good, helpful, and even a good example for others while having on the other side, the "secular life." We have lived in that dichotomy for centuries, and it is time to say that it is wrong and that it is not biblical because, according to the written Word, there is no Christian life and secular life. If you are a disciple of Jesus then you are in whatever place, moment, condition, and activity; and everything you do you must do for the Lord (Colossians 3:23-24).

The phrase "go to church" makes us think that it is a destination to visit, a good place to hang out on certain days of the week. Instead, saying "we are the church" lets us know that we are a part of the church, and we never stop being so, no matter where whe are or whom we are with.

Look at the following text from your Bible:

The God who made the world and everything in it is the Lord of heaven and earth and does not live in temples built by human hands. And he is not served by human hands, as if he needed anything. Rather, he himself gives everyone life and breath and everything else. From one man he made all the nations, that they should inhabit the whole earth; and he marked out their appointed times in history and the boundaries of their lands. God did this so that they would seek him and perhaps reach out for him and find him, though he is not far from any one of us. "For in him we live and move and have our being". As some of your own poets have said, "We are his offspring."
(Acts 17:24-28)

God is not always in the temples, but he is always in the church.

Many find it difficult to understand this phrase because they consider the temple as a synonym for church, but it is not. We are the church! What verse 28 says is compelling: "For in him we live and move and have our being." As some of your own poets have said, 'We are his offspring.' God is in the church, so he dwells in us, and we are a part of his family.

GOD IS NOT ALWAYS IN THE TEMPLES, BUT HE IS ALWAYS IN THE CHURCH.

We gather in temples, yes, but God is not there because of the place, he is there because of us, his church. True disciples never cease to be the church and that is precisely why they are aware that they must be an active part of the meetings. They know how important community life is, they are a part of the body, they relate to others, and they serve God with their gifts and talents. But their mission does not end there. The disciple looks inside themself, examines themself periodically, and renders an account to their discipler based on the growth steps that the individual has taken. For this reason, although one participates in the meetings, **a**

disciple does not depend on the meeting to grow and fulfill what Christ has entrusted to them.

Attending a congregation does not require you to be a disciple but BEING PART of a community of followers of Jesus requires you to be a disciple wherever you are, and requires you to fulfill the mission of making other disciples! No matter what community of believers you belong to, the mission remains the same, and you remain a part of the global church. We are all united in the same faith, purpose, and mission.

This perspective is born from understanding that the church is not a place limited to a physical space, but is a living organism and, as such, must grow integrally, as well as reproduce, multiply, and expand. If this does not happen, it is because we are doing something wrong.

Remember that just being a disciple of Jesus is not God's complete plan for you. It is also necessary to make disciples, model the character of Christ to others, accompany them to live this process, and encourage them to duplicate themselves in others.

PARADIGM SHIFTS:

- I do not attend a church; I AM the church.

- The building where we meet is NOT the church, it is a temple.

- The church is not a static place; it is a LIVING organism.

- The church is made up of the children of God, wherever they come together. Whether that's in a large auditorium, in a park, or in a house, wherever the children of God are, that is where the church is.

IMPLEMENT IDEAS THAT CHANGE THE CULTURE

- Put up posters in the temple with phrases that help everyone change their mindset from "going to church" to "being the Church."

- Try to repeat these phrases several times in meetings until the concepts become part of the habitual language.

- Work with all ministry members and volunteers so that in classes, small group meetings, and even individual counseling it is clearly stated that everything we Christians do every day has to do with the church.

TEACHING AND DISCIPLESHIP ARE NOT THE SAME THING

A Christian understanding of the world sees a child´s character not as genetically determined but as shaped to a significant degree by parental discipleship and discipline.

Russell D. Moore

It is easy to mix up teaching and discipleship because teaching is part of discipleship, but it is essential to differentiate between them. While discipleship uses teaching, teaching alone does not make disciples.

The practical reality of today's Christians is that we are bombarded by an enormous amount of diverse information, messages, and teachings on multiple networks. We have everything, and we idolize those who "speak better" and have popular social followings, but. . . how are we making disciples? Obviously, we don't want to judge anyone's character, but it's good to be clear that speaking well for a limited amount of time in a video or on a pulpit is not the same as doing what Jesus commanded us to do. Discipling is more than just speaking well.

Perhaps the key is not to stay in the discursive part of communication. Both authors of this book worked on this material because we want to help you include personal challenges in your teaching and in that intentional process which we are calling discipleship.

The personal or collective challenges that put into practice what has been learned in a relationship optimize results.

Reflect with your team on these differences between teaching and discipleship:

TEACHING	DISCIPLESHIP
Transmits knowledge.	Transmits a culture.
Is limited to classes and does not require much of a relationship with the teacher.	Aims for accompaniment and requires a relationship with the discipler.
Is based on knowing what the Bible or theology says.	Is based on practicing what the Bible says.
Leads you to greater knowledge.	Leads you to maturity in Christ.
Is a short moment or stage of life aimed to finish a program, training, or class.	Is a process that focuses on one's character.

If you pay attention to this chart, you can see that **discipleship takes much more effort and time than teaching.** Teachers are a key part of the process, but **if you really want to disciple others. You are going to have to move to a new level of commitment and relationship.** The process can start with teaching, but it doesn't end there.

WHOEVER EXERCISES THE INTENTIONAL PROCESS OF DISCIPLESHIP ASSUMES TRAITS OF SPIRITUAL PATERNITY.

Can you be a teacher and not be making disciples? Yes. When you limit teaching to the imparting of information, then the Word becomes a theory, and that conformism prevents God's truth from being real and alive in the person's life.

When you understand this and change the way you teach, then everything you teach will bear more fruit, since it will point toward the goal of making disciples and not just creating clones that know everything you already know. Additionally, at the end of the road, we are sure that you will be taught by each disciple too, because you never stop being one!

Someone who disciples is much more than a teacher. Little by little they become an example of life, a counselor, a coach, and a friend. Whoever exercises the intentional process of discipleship assumes traits of spiritual paternity since they assign identity, provide, and protect.

PARADIGM SHIFTS

- Teaching is not the "whole point" of discipleship.

- The driving force of discipleship is the relationships, not the knowledge.

- Knowing the Bible does not bring maturity; living it does.

IMPLEMENT IDEAS THAT CHANGE THE CULTURE

- Begin to differentiate biblical classes from discipleship processes.

- Instruct all involved (leaders, volunteers, and participants) to understand the difference.

- Identify those in your congregation who can be disciplers and train them with this guide.

- Make sure that all classes point to changes of action that will be monitored in a relationship.

EVERY DISCIPLE IS DIFFERENT

Fortunately, God made all varieties of people with a wide variety of interests and abilities. He has called people of every race and color who have been hurt by life in every manner imaginable. Even the scars of past abuse and injury can be the means of bringing healing to another. What wonderful opportunities to make disciples!.

Charles R. Swindoll

The Greek philosophy that we inherited in the West from the Roman Empire gave us the not-so-astute idea that education should be like a funnel through which we all go in differently and then we all come out the same. Some have unknowingly sought this type of approach for discipleship and the church.

For this reason, programs are created with the expectation that every believer can complete them and become the same as all other Christians. However, today it is clear that we are all the same in essence, but we are all unique and we must all be brought to discipleship. Recognizing this is a good thing! Every disciple is different, has specific needs, and struggles with things that others don't. Their strengths and weaknesses are unique, and it is not possible to create a program that can serve everyone equally.

EVERY DISCIPLE IS DIFFERENT, HAS SPECIFIC NEEDS, AND STRUGGLES WITH THINGS THAT OTHERS DON'T.

In turn, the disciplers are aware of their own weaknesses in order to depend more on Christ, assume their strengths to be imparted to their followers, and are all fully guided by the Spirit of God.

It is for this reason that discipleship is more about personal development than just a collective group development. The group and the individual must be two complementary parts because it is not one or the other but both. There are truths that are better learned communally and others that must be taught face-to-face in the intimacy of two people. The challenge is that almost all church programs are made up of a big or small collective of people and there is little one-on-one approach. This is why it is so vital to remember that **intimate conversations, personal encounters, and one-on-one challenges are a mark of genuine discipleship.**

Some ideas to disciple on a personal level:

- Don't look at numbers, look at people.

- Create opportunities that go outside of a class setting.

- Create appropriate intentional intimacy as opposed to waiting for it to come naturally.

- Find out the interests of each disciple.

- If you want a genuine relationship, be authentic.

- Invest more into those who show greater interest and enthusiasm.

- Teach them to be accountable for their lives. This is imperative.

- Celebrate their successes, comfort them in their setbacks.

- Work on specific actions.

- Help them set/focus on personal goals.

- Assist them in depending on the Holy Spirit to be their guide.

These tips will vary slightly if you are discipling children, preteens, teens, or young adults. Each of the following principles will assist you in discovering the superior point of focus for each of the age groups. There is, however, no age limitation for someone to become a disciple.

PARADIGM SHIFTS

- To God we are all equal, but we are also different and unique.

- Discipleship always becomes a personal relationship.

- The weekly meetings do not disciple; the relationship does.

- We were created in the image and likeness of a multiform God.

IMPLEMENT IDEAS THAT CHANGE THE CULTURE

- Know the individual differences of the people who are in your discipleship group.

- Intentionally be aware of which paradigm is important to transfer value to them.

- Help the people you disciple get to know each other better.

- Create a conscious awareness of inclusion and integration in the members of your projects.

- Model a personalized pastoral approach.

DISCIPLESHIP IS FOR EVERY AGE

Jesus spent time and had close and personal relationships with his disciples. Do we have personal relationships with the new generations in our churches?

La Verne Tolbert

It seems that the general conscience of many congregations demands that we "seriously" disciple adults, while children, preteens, teens, and young adults can wait, and this is a strategic error with dire consequences. In fact, when it comes to transmitting culture, the best age is the youngest. When you work with adults you will find that it is a little more difficult to change something that they have done in a certain and determined way for their entire lives. Instead, the youngest are moldable, teachable, and adaptable. They know that they don't know, and that's good.

If you have an influential position with the new generations, God has held you in high esteem.

Now, working with children is not the same as working with young adults, so here are some recommendations that correspond to the 4 basic work areas of an intelligent vision for generational pastoral care.

WHEN IT COMES TO TRANSMITTING CULTURE, THE BEST AGE IS THE YOUNGEST.

FOR THE DISCIPLESHIP OF CHILDREN

- Work closely with parents. They are the natural leaders and disciplers that God gave children. Discipling children is cooperating with their parents.

- Help children share their growth steps in the context of their family.

- Use multiple sources, so the training process will be comprehensive and will reach everyone. (If you want to know more about multiple intelligences, take advantage of the course at the e625 online Institute.)

FOR THE DISCIPLESHIP OF PRETEENS

- This is the stage where we begin to see the world beyond just the home and with the arrival of abstract thought we begin to question the validity of what we learned in childhood. For this reason, teaching must move from concrete data to abstract principles.

- At this stage it is also crucial to collaborate with their parents because this is the last great opportunity they will have to shape desired values and habits in their children. In the following stages of their lives, instilling values becomes more difficult.

- The relationship with their leaders and teachers must now be more personal. They need models and it is very possible that the models they have at this stage will continue to subconsciously be their example for the rest of their lives.

FOR THE DISCIPLESHIP OF TEENS

- The relationship of boys and girls with their parents is always important, but the relationship with their friends at this age is key. Communal discipleship is most significant at this stage.

- Naturally, in adolescence we all question our family framework and leaders should not throw more fuel on the fire but rather help them positively make that evaluation.

- Be prepared to talk with them about feelings and emotions. Their life during this stage is going to be a roller coaster of emotional ups and downs and they will need someone mature, and therefore stable, to accompany them.

FOR THE DISCIPLESHIP OF YOUNG ADULTS

- To the same degree that communal discipleship is vital in the previous stage, mentorship is vital in this young adult phase. A mentor meets their deepest needs and allows space to ask difficult questions, even the most intimate questions.

- Present options to young adults without giving them orders and, above all, without making decisions for them. Teach them to make their decisions based on the Word of God. Coaching is a good discipline to add to your skills and in the e625.com online institute you can find foundational generational coaching courses.

- In this stage, most consider pursuing a profession, choosing a marriage partner, planning for the future, and discovering one's life purpose (or even a ministerial calling). These are the talking points in the discipleship relationship with young adults.

PARADIGM SHIFTS

- Age is not a limitation to making disciples, but it is necessary to adapt according to the stage.

- Discipling adults is not more valuable than discipling little ones.

- The transferring of culture takes time, focus, and effort.

IMPLEMENT IDEAS THAT CHANGE THE CULTURE

- Work on a vision of *Generational Leadership.*[1] (If you haven't read this book we recommend you do so as soon as possible.) Join the adult ministries with those in your congregation who are dedicated to the new generations and plan an activity that focuses on making the discipleship of new generations a priority for your entire church, as it was commissioned by God in Deuteronomy 6. Coordinating efforts from time to time does wonders for the heart and minds of co-laborers.

- Organize things in a way that each of the new generational stages lead a meeting one or more times per year. Give preteens responsibilities, encourage teens to be an example for the little ones, train young adults to model behavior in teens, and provide examples of maturity to take firm steps toward the next stage in which they find themselves.

---

1. Lucas Leys. *Liderazgo Generacional.* (Dallas, Texas: Editorial e625, 2017).

PRINCIPLE 5

DISCIPLESHIP HAPPENS IN PROCESSES

When the church becomes an end in itself, it ends.
When any ministry, no matter how great, becomes an
end goal, it ends. What we need is for discipleship to
become the goal, and then the process of conversion and
sanctification will never end.
Robby Gallaty

When we talk about discipling others, we must consider how to elevate our disciples' level of maturity. It is about going from one point to the next. This makes it necessary to draw a route that marks the steps of that sustained growth that we seek, while understanding that there are smaller steps along the way. When we understand this better, we focus less on our own assessment of events and pay more attention to a progressive view of processes.

It is one thing to learn a principle and quite another to live it. The first is an intellectual act, something that can be received in a class. To put a principle into practice, however, requires decision, effort, and the fulfillment of goals that help make the principle a part of our culture and way of life.

For this reason, someone who decides to disciple cannot be satisfied with teaching principles, since that is only the first part. It is necessary that these principles

WE FOCUS LESS ON OUR OWN ASSESSMENT OF EVENTS AND PAY MORE ATTENTION TO A PROGRESSIVE VIEW OF PROCESSES.

are part of the discipler's culture so that they can transmit them in such a way that they become part of the culture of the disciple.

It is a lifestyle that should arise naturally and not be forced.

THE PENTAGON OF LEARNING APPLIED TO DISCIPLESHIP

The book *Generational Leadership* describes the need to improve teaching methods from a relational nuance with the following pentagon:

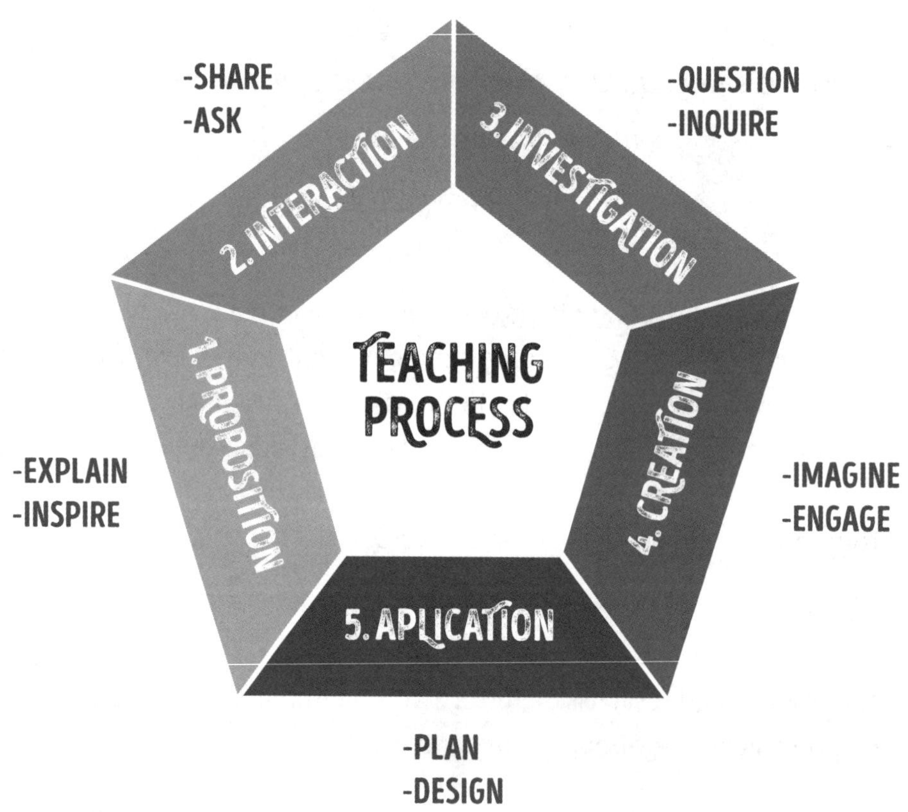

© 2017 Lucas Leys

Each one of the sides of the pentagon marks a dimension of the action that the disciplers must observe. If you think about it well, you will understand the need to make disciples through processes, instead of just having students in a class.

Here's an example of how this process works:

1. **PROPOSITION:** Pick an aspect of the character of Christ.

2. **INTERACTION:** Explore the different appreciations of the aspect.

3. **INVESTIGATION:** Look up what the Bible says about it.

4. **CREATION:** Engage others in doing it together.

5. **APPLICATION:** Live it in your own flesh and be accountable for it.

A process can be focused on a specific area of the disciple's life, on a specific theme, on an aspect of character, etc., so that in the same way you can create different proposals for stages that adapt to the principles of this pentagon. Nothing is rigid. On the contrary, everything is adaptable and 100 percent improvable and you can read more in the book *Generational Leadership*.

Although this book may appear to speak to the project of making disciples, it is meant as a tool to help guide a long-term process whose final goal is to form the character of Christ in the life of the believer, which is entirely dependent on the relationship between discipler and disciple and their mutual commitment to the process.

PARADIGM SHIFTS

- Discipleship is not a propositional discourse but a process of internalizing truths that respect the different abilities of our brains to learn.

- The preacher shares a monologue, the teacher teaches a class, the discipler accompanies through stages.

- The relationship between disciplers and disciples is the very nature of discipleship.

IMPLEMENT IDEAS THAT CHANGE THE CULTURE

- Get used to creating processes. Preaching or lectures are not as effective in generating understanding for most people. Use series, long-term lessons, and various instances so that different people internalize the contents of what you want them to practice.

- The call is not to have meetings where we stand to sing and then listen to a lecture. Think outside the sanctuary, the classroom, and the speeches given.

PRINCIPLE 6

ACCOMPANIMENT AND MENTORSHIP

I believe in the transforming power of the Spirit of God and that Jesus can be formed in the life of the new generations. I work from his reality, not from fiction.

Félix Ortiz

According to what we can notice in the New Testament, the apostle Paul would come to a city, preach, and then continue working with a few select believers until he formed in them the character of Christ so that they would then do the same with others. When it was time, he left there but he did not disconnect from them: he continued to give them instructions through his writings.

If we are talking about relationships and processes, we must consider the development of relationships in phases or stages and that is why it is good to include the word *project*. If we want to form disciples with maturity, who truly reflect the character of Christ, we must first form the attributes of Christ in ourselves and then gradually develop each aspect of our personal commitments, modeling them in the lives of others. Paul said: "Be imitators of me, just as I am of Christ" and this can take years. At the same time, it is advisable to plant it with phases and times, and then release the disciples so that they go and repeat the process with others.

THE GREATEST WEALTH OF DISCIPLESHIP IS IN THE RELATIONSHIP.

The relationship with your disciples can last a lifetime, and they may even perceive you as a spiritual reference, but that does not necessarily mean that the roles are eternal and that they will not grow past it. The point is to accompany them in this stage to help them take the mature steps they need to take in this period in which they find themselves. This "staying in touch" can use digital tools such as video chats, social media, and similar tools. But the point is to mentor, that is, model to transfer certain vital lessons that must be learned at a stage in life.

Look what the book of Exodus says about God's relationship with Moses. Although Moses could not look directly into the face of God because he would have died, his personal encounter with the Eternal God produced in him a weight of glory that others could not fail to recognize.

The Lord would speak to Moses face to face, as one speaks to a friend. Then Moses would return to the camp, but his young aide Joshua son of Nun did not leave the tent.
(Exodus 33:11)

In other words, being close to a good role model has an impact that sooner or later everyone will notice. Moses was discipled by God, just as all of us can be. This process is based on the relationship we reach with him. In the same way, we can all accompany others in their growth process.

PARADIGM SHIFTS

- There is no discipleship without accompaniment.

- The greatest wealth of discipleship is in the relationship.

- The discipleship relationship can last a lifetime, although roles usually change according to the stages of life.

IMPLEMENT IDEAS THAT CHANGE THE CULTURE

- Take personal time with each person you have in a discipleship group.

- Let the people in your group know aspects of your life that are outside of a weekly class.

- They should keep in mind from early on that one day they will have to disciple others. Thus, the change will not be left alone in your hands, since the responsibility of making disciples belongs to all believers.

- Create projects for specific stages of life with measurable results.

PARENTS' INVOLVEMENT

We discipline our children not so that they will make us happy, but so that they will serve Christ as adults. We educate them not so they can have a good job, but to develop them to be the best follower of Jesus that they can be.
Chap Bettis

All Christian parents are involved in the discipleship of their children even if they don't know it or are unintentional about it. The job of every church leader is to make sure parents know this and help them to be intentional about doing it better.

As children grow, their ability and need to relate to other role models also grows. That is where we come in, not as something parallel to the family but rather by joining forces in a collaborative way. The point is that a constant interaction between leadership and parents goes much further than we might suspect. The role of the parents decreases as the children grow older and it is necessary for this to happen, because otherwise, they could never become mature children who effectively serve the kingdom of heaven. But again. . . this is a PROCESS. It could be slow moving, and we must be patient, but that is why, when we work

ALL CHRISTIAN PARENTS ARE INVOLVED IN THE DISCIPLESHIP OF THEIR CHILDREN EVEN IF THEY DON'T KNOW IT

on discipleship from the perspective of the church, we need to nurture a positive relationship with parents as well.

The role of each one could vary over time, in this way:

6–9	10–13	14–17	18–25

6–9

- Children are discipled by their parents.
- Parents are the clearest role model.
- Leaders support parents' leadership.
- Their contact with preteens is vital.

10–13

- Parents are important role models, as are leaders and teachers.
- Parents should get other adults to support their work.
- Their contact with positive teens is vital.

14–17

- Parents model.
- Leaders are mentors.
- Parents should relate with their children's friends.
- Contact with young adults who are good role models is vital.

18–25

- Parents and leaders delegate autonomy.
- Leaders must be life mentors and coaches for specific decisions.
- Contact with young married couples with good relationships is vital.

PARADIGM SHIFTS

- The role of parents changes as the ages advance.
- Leaders without the parents can't get very far.

- The parents must learn to lean on leaders.

IMPLEMENT IDEAS THAT CHANGE THE CULTURE

- Set a good pace for parent meetings based on the age of your students.

- Promote parent-child meetings more often. The interaction that this highlight God's design for the church.

- As a disciple, you must always think of each disciple within a family context. There will always be people close to you who can be a good influence on the development of the one you are discipling.

- Let non-Christian parents know that the church is there to help them in their parenthood.

PRINCIPLE 8

THE MIRROR PRINCIPLE

Discipleship is the process of becoming who Jesus would be if He were you.
Dallas Willard

The apostle John made this principle clear: "Whoever claims to live in him must live as Jesus did" (1 John 2:6).

The first great commitment of those of us who dedicate ourselves to the discipleship project is to reflect Christ in everything: his character, passion, decisions, will, and transparency. That is why it is said that no one can disciple if they are not a disciple first. Anyone who is willing to be a disciple tries to look more like Jesus every day since he came, in turn, to reflect the Father. As Paul says, Christ is the image of the invisible God (Colossians 1:15).

The second great commitment is to extend this for others to also resemble Jesus. For this reason we have an exciting and enormous responsibility that can sometimes intimidate us, for which we must also learn from Jesus's dependence on God. In John 15:15 we find him saying: "I no longer call you servants, because a servant does not know his master's business. Instead, I have called you friends, for everything that I learned from my Father I have made known to you."

How good to know that we have a great and powerful God and that he continually renews his mercy for us because we will need it in this process. If we depend on him in the discipleship project, we will surely succeed!

If you think about it, you will see that creation has that same design. Everything that God created has his stamp of ownership. Everything resembles him. Everything was made by him, through him, and for him. Genesis tells the story of the creation of the human being, saying that they were made "in the image and likeness of God" That is, they were created as a mirror that reflects him and starting from this principle, we could design a discipleship process as follows:

1. I know one aspect of the character of Christ. For example: love.

2. I long to be like him in that way.

3. I stop loving my way, to start loving as he loved.

4. I battle against the arguments that prevent me from loving as he loved.

5. I live and practice his love.

6. I teach others to love like him.

7. I choose another aspect of Christ's character to imitate...and so the whole process begins again.

In this way, the discipleship process will last a lifetime, because in each aspect we can find a new depth in the next stage. It is good to be able to work on it with those we have been put in charge of.

PARADIGM SHIFTS

- Reflecting Jesus in our own lives is more important than giving a good sermon or class about Jesus. That means dying to myself so that he can live in me.

- All creation was made in the image of God, and we must and can recover that design.

- Reflecting Christ is not a feeling or a romantic lyric to a cute song but a concrete action in which you model his character.

IMPLEMENT IDEAS THAT CHANGE THE CULTURE

- Choose specific aspects of Jesus's character to reflect on, understand, and develop.

- Prepare a progressive and ordered teaching plan. Put up signs that say something like: "This is the month of love." You can use videos and images for this purpose, and testimonies can be given about experiences of giving and receiving love, so that everyone involved in the discipleship project is clear about the tangible objective that is being worked on.

REFLECTING CHRIST IS NOT A FEELING OR A ROMANTIC LYRIC TO A CUTE SONG BUT A CONCRETE ACTION IN WHICH YOU MODEL HIS CHARACTER.

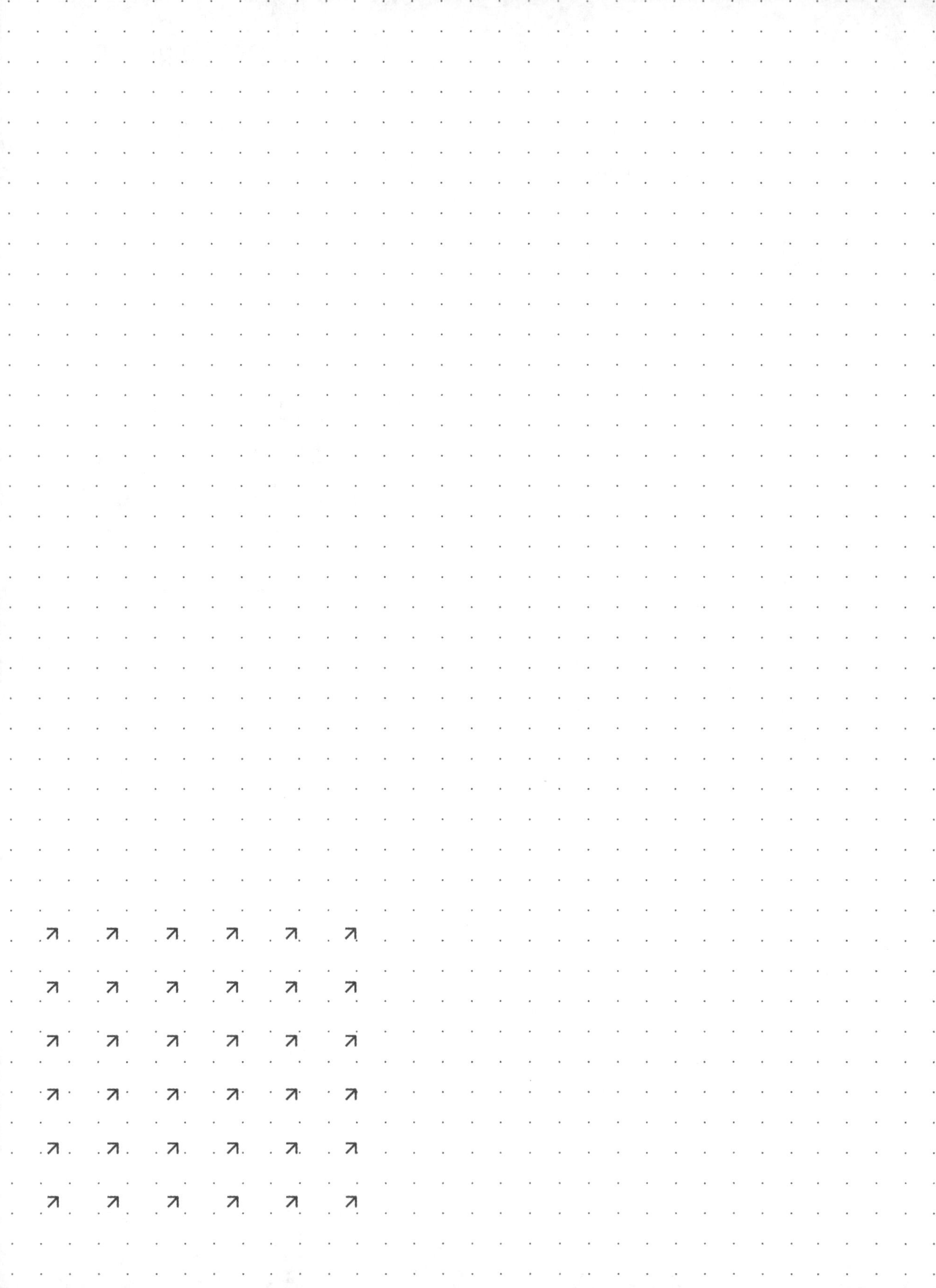

PRINCIPLE 9

ACTIVITIES WITH A PURPOSE

Renewing ourselves is not a luxury, it is a necessity for every follower of Jesus in order to continue being agents of restoration and reconciliation in a broken world.

Félix Ortiz

When we mentally leave behind the sanctuary, the classroom, and the liturgy, our panorama expands to the point that we find new scenarios and possibilities to achieve the great purpose of discipleship, which is that the people we influence become more like Jesus.

For the best disciplers, everything is done with a purpose, both relationships and spontaneous conversations at every available opportunity, as well as good programs that facilitate the internalization of desired behaviors.

Some of these activities will be personal or relationship building for a small group. Others, however, should include the community. This is how we teach kids, pre-teens, teens, and young adults to be one body. There, character problems will also be revealed, and they will learn to support each other. Then, the disciples will be aware of the reactions of the disciplers to continue forming Christ in them, and the disciplers will also keep an eye on their disciples to imitate them. In those situations, you will realize that they look at you more than you realize.

Remember that it is not about creative ideas just to be creative, or spectacular activities with the desire to be spectacular. From the point of view of the disciple, even the spectacle of a program is simply a pedagogical tool (and not for

LET US ASK GOD FOR WISDOM TO ENSURE THAT EACH ACTIVITY IS ALIGNS WITH HIS INTENTIONS FOR OUR MINISTRIES.

you to show off). The basic objectives are to promote coexistence, create interest, and facilitate practical lessons in which to model principles.

Think of all these activities from the perspectives of the purpose of discipleship and you will find a new dimension to them:

- Going for a walk outside

- Playing sports

- Climbing a mountain

- Going swimming

- Planting or caring for a tree or plant

- Reading a book

- Visiting the sick, elderly, or orphans

- Watching a movie

- Going to the theater, circus, dance, etc.

- Carrying out a carpentry project

- Playing or singing a song that you can discuss together

- Visiting a relative

The possibilities are endless.

Let us ask God for wisdom to ensure that each activity aligns with his intentions for our ministries.

PARADIGM SHIFTS

- Exercise, play, and fellowship are excellent ministry tools when done with a purpose.

- The activities planned outside the sanctuary are as rich and necessary as those that take place inside.

- Discipleship is not reduced to listening, but they must see and act. That is why it is necessary to create these moments with our programs.

IMPLEMENT IDEAS THAT CHANGE THE CULTURE

- Plan for the long term and share the plan with everyone you can.

- Present a public report of all the activities you facilitate outside the sanctuary. It is always better when everyone finds out about the riches that are achieved in personal discipleship.

- Insistently convey to everyone involved in your ministry the idea that your mission is not for them to listen to a biblical proposition quietly and just say amen. It promotes a culture of coexistence, actions, and experiences and not only of sermons and classes.

THE CALL IS FOR EVERYONE

Discipleship is not a choice.
Tim Keller

To think that only pastors have the call to disciple others is nonsense. The great commission to go and make disciples (Matthew 28:16-20; Mark 16:14-18; Luke 24:36-49; and John 20:19-23) was given to all the disciples.

If we acknowledge Jesus as our Lord and Savior, then we have a call to discipleship.

All Christians must disciple and doing so is one of the most tremendous ways we can grow because we all learn by teaching. We have all received something that we can give and have learned something that we can teach. Along the way, some are filled with fear or justifications, thinking that they must prepare a lot or that they could make a mistake. But the reality is that we are all in the process of learning because we never stop being disciples, and of course we are going to make mistakes. That is neither something new, nor is it a tragedy.

If Christ trusts us for this task, it must be because we can do it.

If the church continues to believe that one sermon is enough to make disciples, then we will continue to see burnt-out pastors and continue to turn good preachers into celebrities because they speak well, even if they don't help us achieve what God wants us to achieve. God wants disciples and not people with good

IF WE ACKNOWLEDGE JESUS AS OUR LORD AND SAVIOR, THEN WE HAVE A CALL TO DISCIPLESHIP.

morals and some biblical knowledge to behave like Christians in the temple on the weekend.

Disciples.

The sermons, the songs, and the temple are tools and not objectives and when they are used well, they help us to produce disciples of Jesus. And the great news is that there are other tools and mechanisms modeled by Jesus himself to achieve it.

This is where the most important action of all appears: being a model. Modeling is something that adults and even young adults always do for the new generations even if we are not aware that we are doing it. The entire proposal of Generational Leadership is linked to this reality and invites us to be intentional with it. All Christian adults are involved in the discipleship of the youth although perhaps without knowing it. The young adults are ready to disciple the teens because they are already modeling for them what the next stage is all about and the teens, in turn, are doing the same with the preteens and the preteens are being watched by the kids. Modeling a natural process, and it is much more effective when we are aware of it and do it with devotion, wit, and fidelity.

PARADIGM SHIFTS

- Discipleship is the task of all God's children.

- Pastors and leaders who do not move everyone to disciple sooner or later will burn out or become superficial, or both.

- Discipleship is something that we may already be doing without realizing it, but that we can improve exponentially if we start doing it intentionally.

IMPLEMENT IDEAS THAT CHANGE THE CULTURE

- The importance of discipleship must be communicated privately, publicly, and continually.

- Delegate authority and don't just focus on your work team and volunteers.

- Celebrate what God celebrates and not what the world already celebrates (such as fame, recognition, beauty, or eloquence).

- Involve new generations in ministry and discipleship at an early age. They are already looking at us.

10 LESSONS FOR DISCIPLING CHILDREN

The childhood stage is a foundational stage, and we are obliged to accompany them in a wise way, since when we disciple children, we are strengthening the bases of character and values that will govern their lives in the future. Each lesson that is discussed with them, each meeting, each mentoring and accompaniment space, must be an intentional moment to affirm their life and their basic ideas regarding life on the rock that is Christ.

The following lessons are designed under the sequence or model "AFFIRM" which uses the process developed in the following acrostic:

 **A**valanche of ideas

 **F**oundations of the theme

 **F**ocus on truth

 **I**ntrospection

 **R**eflect on a character

 **M**obilize

This AFFIRM model facilitates a discipleship process in which both teachers and each learner are challenged to grow and mature.

These are details for each stage:

1. **Avalanche of ideas.** Here we will carry out activities that help children to begin to think about the proposed topic. These will not be isolated activities, or simple icebreakers, but part of a whole within the process.

2. **Foundations of the theme.** It is a compendium of theoretical foundations that help us clarify ideas and generate biblical, scientific, and philosophical support on the proposed topic.

3. **Focus on truth.** This section contains the necessary biblical support to train children in the principles of the Word of God and approach the subject from a biblical perspective. All the lessons point to the fact that they can find the answers to all the problems of life in Scripture.

4. **Introspection.** In this portion we will give the children short sentences that allow us to synthesize what we want them to learn. At each opportunity you can recite the phrase to them and repeat it throughout the week so that the children learn it. Each sentence summarizes the core of the lesson that we want them to remember forever!

5. **Reflect on a character.** In this section we will reflect with the children on two characters. The first will be a fantasy character known to the children, and then we will introduce them to a biblical character. In both cases they will be asked to assess whether this character has qualities to be a role model, either positive or negative.

6. **Mobilize.** At this point the idea is to generate a list of specific actions that will be taken by the discipler and the disciple to be executed after finishing the lesson. The intention is that the subject matter does not remain a blurry memory, but that we can mobilize each boy and girl to put into practice what they have learned. This section will

also motivate you to contact the parents of the children so you can work together with them.

This same sequence will also help you to create other topics and lessons, or to enhance other materials that you can access on www.e625.com.

And remember: discipleship is a long-term process.

BIG IDEA!

Ask each one of the participants in this process to get a notebook or journal to work in and figure out if they can afford it themselves or if you can raise the money to buy them all one with the parents' help and give it to them as a gift with your ministry's logo on it.

You could call it DISCIPLE'S JOURNAL. In it, the boys and girls will be able to take notes, draw pictures, write their ideas, and also write down and render accounts of what they plan to do during the week, thus obtaining good coordination between parents, disciples, and disciplers. This idea is useful so that these lessons do not simply remain in attending classes, but that this is a true discipleship process that produces genuine growth in the new generations! Ask their parents to get involved with the children in decorating this journal, so that it is compatible with the taste of each boy and girl.

(Have free notebooks and extra paper for when new children arrive, or someone does not bring their journal.)

PREVIOUS TRAINING FOR DISCIPLERS

We assume that you have come this far having read Section 1 of this material, but just in case, and just to be sure, in the first part of this book we tell you that you have the training guide for those who take on the challenge of discipling the new generations.

A discipler can be a leader of the children's group, a leader of a small group, or a Sunday school teacher, but it can also be any person who has been trained and authorized by the pastoral ministry for the exercise of discipleship. In fact, parents are the first ones called to disciple their children.

This project tries to mobilize more people to take up the challenge of not continuing to sit in religious comfort, but to be of help to the new generations, just as Christ designed, from season to season, in and out of the sanctuaries, inside and outside of meetings.

BEFORE WE START

Now that you are about to start this discipleship project for children, it would be good for you to consider certain guidelines.

IF YOU'RE A PARENT OF ONE OR MORE CHILDREN...

This material is designed to work in a small group of boys and girls. The ideal number could be between 6 and 10 participants per group (and if you have more, break them into small groups incorporating other leaders in the process). You could create a group with your children and others who live close by and are already friends with them. However, if you want to work with only your children in this process but don't have a group, you can tailor each lesson by modifying the group activities a bit to work with a smaller number of participants, or just not do them at all. In any case, we recommend you read the entire lesson, study it, and prepare several days in advance.

You should also set a date and time to be able to have meetings every week. It is not convenient to work the lessons in an accelerated way, but once a week would be fine, and perhaps even once every two weeks. That will depend on the consistency of the group or the way you organize your family.

IF YOU'RE A TEACHER OR LEADER OF CHILDREN...

Preparation is fundamental, and it multiplies the percentage of good results in the discipleship process.

The material in this book is designed for meetings that can last between 60 and 90 minutes. However, you can adapt the lessons to last as long as you need, according to the time you have available.

If you are going to use this material for Sunday school classes (or whatever name your church prefers), you will need to adapt the lesson for the duration of that space. You could cut out any of the sections or certain activities can be done at home. For that, the DISCIPLE'S JOURNAL may be of great help. A simple notebook where they can make notes, keep track of their progress, and even write down tasks and personal goals, will give continuity to the process. You can also use it to stay in touch with the parents of your children.

ADAPT AND ENRICH THIS MATERIAL

Each lesson contains all the information you need to teach participants about the proposed topic. However, it is always advisable to increase, decrease, or change details if you consider it necessary because nobody knows your group as well as you do.

Although it is true that the most common timeframe we have to work with children is during Sunday school (which lasts approximately 40 to 50 minutes), this is not the only opportunity we have to disciple. You can call a meeting on another day of the week, or even make a virtual meeting. Don't be limited by tradition!

Important: The time you spend on each part of the lesson will depend on what you have scheduled. If you have less time, you can shorten some of the longer parts. In any case, we suggest you don't just remove any part.

It is better that they have the full experience in small portions, than just a fleeting and superficial teaching that they will later forget.

Some extra ideas to enrich the lessons are:

- **Music:** Music moves hearts, and with children it is no exception. Use a choreographed song to start and end each lesson. This way the children will begin and end the meeting connected and with a ready spirit.

- **Invite guests:** Don't think that the entire burden of the meeting should always fall on you. Occasionally invite some teenagers or preteens to support you in songs, with costumes, to tell stories, or simply to share the moment.

- **Go at your own pace:** You don't need to rush and do it all at once. If you consider the information important, you can divide it into two weeks or more. If you do the first 3 points one week, the next week you can do the other 3. Just make sure you put together a creative and varied learning process each time.

- **Be creative:** Awaken the imagination of the little ones. Use all the senses you can at every opportunity! Do not use the material as something rigid, but adapt it to your needs.

We wish you the best in this adventure! Have a spectacular start in this beautiful task of making disciples from childhood!

LESSON 1

WHO IS A DISCIPLE?

Transformation is a process, a journey, not a one-time decision and the sooner it starts, the better.

David Kinnaman

Who is a disciple?

Depending on the age of your boys and girls and how long they've been in church, you may be able to get some of them to tell you that "a disciple is an apprentice or a student" or "they are someone who follows Jesus" and so on. But the objective of this discipleship project is that when hearing that question, they can answer: "I am."

The goal of this material is to be able to help each boy and girl to identify themselves as disciples. It will be of no use to them to know what the word means if they do not identify with it and experience it.

For this reason, the aim is that the boys and girls in your discipleship group not only learn what a disciple is, but that they can become disciples for the rest of their lives. This is where we start the project.

AVALANCHE OF IDEAS

Introductory activities are ideal for connecting the group with the topic to be discussed. This time we will start with an activity that we will call "The Apprentices."

Remember that each activity must be planned considering the age of your group. If you have nine-ten-year-old children you can use more complex elements and activities, and if your group is six-year-old boys and girls you should use more basic elements according to their level. In any case, the proposed activity can be adapted to different ages so that it can be carried out in any group.

ACTIVITY: THE APPRENTICES

Plan a kitchen scenario. You can create "Chef Graseoli's Kitchen" or come up with any other funny name for them. During the activity, you will be that character. Wear a chef costume, with a very striking hat. You can also wear a big mustache, like those of the typical Italian chef. Or maybe you choose to be a refined and exquisite French chef. They can speak in an exaggerated and funny way, and with some special accent (Italian, French, or another). Turn on suitable music so that it also helps create the atmosphere you want.

Get some aprons too, or ask parents to send an apron with their children to the meeting. This must be planned in advance.

The idea for this activity is that you have well-defined instructions of what you want to teach them, and that they can feel as if they were real chef apprentices. That environment will be generated by you.

Choose something you want to teach your group. Some ideas are:

- Bring cookies and teach them how to decorate them with icing.

- Have everyone bring some chopped fruit to make a big fruit salad. You can add cream to give it a special touch.

ADVICE

- Get into character. The more appealing it is to them, the more they will enjoy the activity.

- The food is not the important part. It doesn't matter so much if they make great designs or not; rather it's about creating relational contact with them.

- Speaking to them as the chef character you invented, highlight positive qualities in them. Tell them that their designs are amazing, and that they are great learners!

During the development of the activity, give them simple instructions to follow. For example, you can tell them that Chef Graseoli is looking for trainees to do the following:

- Whenever they talk to the chef, they will call them by name (Chef Graseoli).

- When they receive a compliment, they should say: "Thank you, Chef Graseoli."

- When something gets dirty or falls, they must clean it up or pick it up immediately.

- They must do everything Chef Graseoli does, as they are the apprentices.

During the activity, repeat to them several times that they are your learners and that they are excellent at learning and following instructions. It highlights the fact that they are now disciples of Chef Graseoli and that in the future they could have a great career as chefs. The activity ends with a big round of applause and a lot of cheering: applause for the chef, applause for them, etc.

Another way to carry out this activity is to ask another adult with love for theater to help play this character. You could then introduce "this famous chef who has come to visit to teach us how to prepare one of their delicious dishes." Remember, the key is not that they make the best design, but that they feel part of a group that welcomes them and that they enjoy the activity.

While everyone eats the cookies, the fruit salad, or whatever you have chosen to prepare, ask them how they felt and what their experience was in learning to cook.

- What did you think of Chef Graseoli?

- Who followed the instructions best?

- Of all the apprentices, which one do you think will be the best chef in the future?

And now announce to them that today we are going to talk about who is a disciple.

📝 FOUNDATIONS OF THE THEME

This section is for you, although you will also be able to translate some foundational ideas to the children in your class. Once again, consider their age to adapt each of the sections to their needs and abilities.

The principle of being instructed, taught, or trained is shown in the Holy Scriptures in Hebrew words like *limmud* or *lamad*, or the Greek word *mathetes*. All these words point to the same thing: actions that lead someone to get used to doing something they didn't do before. This is very important. In the simplest sense, it refers to creating a habit that you didn't have before and not just understanding a truth.

The word "disciple" in the Hebrew culture is said with the word *talmid*, so a *talmid* (disciple) has the goal of being *lamad* (instructed), to create habits that they did not have before and that help them resemble their teacher.

At this point it is convenient that, as a discipler, you ask yourself the following questions:

How can I be a better imitator of Jesus? What habits should I add to my life?

That is what being a disciple and being a discipler is all about: someone who learns closely from a teacher and attracts others to learn as well. If we imitate Jesus, we are his disciples, and if we do it well, we will attract others to be as well.

Teach your kids that:

- The Hebrew word for disciples is *talmid* (the point is not that they know a Hebrew word but that you teach them to think beyond what they know).

- A disciple is someone who is willing to learn.

- A disciple imitates the Master in everything they do.

- A disciple of Jesus seeks to become more and more like Jesus.

📖 FOCUS ON TRUTH

Get some posters or papers to serve as examples of what you are teaching. Audio-visual aids are useful at any age, but especially when we work with children since by God's design, they can be visual or audio learners. Because of this, visual aids help children understand better and it is ideal to use visible examples when words, situations, or concepts appear that they do not know.

Look at the following list together.

What does the Bible tell us about what Jesus was like?

- He loved people.
  "As the Father has loved me, so have I loved you. Now remain in my love." (John 15:9)

- He was compassionate.
  "When he saw the crowds, he had compassion on them, because they were harassed and helpless, like sheep without a shepherd." (Matthew 9:36)

- He was gentle and humble.

  "Take my yoke upon you and learn from me, for I am gentle and humble in heart, and you will find rest for your soul." (Matthew 11:29)

- He was obedient to his Father.

  "Father, if you are willing, take this cup from me; yet not my will, but yours be done." (Luke 22:42)

- He was honest.

  "They sent their disciples to him along with the Herodians. 'Teacher,' they said, 'we know that you are a man of integrity and that you teach the way of God in accordance with the truth. You aren't swayed by others, because you pay no attention to who they are." (Matthew 22:16)

- He prayed all the time.

  "Yet the news about him spread all the more, so that crowds of people came to hear him and to be healed of their sicknesses. But Jesus often withdrew to lonely places and prayed". (Luke 5:15-16)

- He denounced evil.

  "'It is written,' he said to them, 'My house will be a house of prayer'; but you have made it 'a den of robbers." (Luke 19:46)

- He served others.

  "The Son of Man did not come to be served, but to serve, and to give his life as a ransom for many." (Matthew 20:28)

- He knew the Word of God well.

  "Jesus went throughout Galilee, teaching in their synagogues, proclaiming the good news of the kingdom, and healing every disease and sickness among the people." (Matthew 4:23)

- He gave hope.

  "The thief comes only to steal and kill and destroy; I have come that they may have life, and have it to the full." (John 10:10)

Ask your children to reflect on these characteristics aloud and have some of them (or all of them, depending on the number) choose two that they want to imitate.

Then remind everyone that our goal as disciples is to become more like Jesus, and that this list will help us do that. (We will return to this list in the last part of this lesson.)

OUR GOAL AS DISCIPLES IS TO BECOME MORE LIKE JESUS.

 # INTROSPECTION

Encourage the group to repeat this phrase with you:

The more I look like Jesus, the better disciple I become.

This is a phrase that you can use several times during the development of this lesson. The sentence summarizes all the content of the lesson, and if there is one thing that you want the boys and girls to remember after each lesson, it is precisely what this sentence summarizes.

Of course, it will not be enough for you to repeat the phrase to them. Have them repeat it and not necessarily only with literal words but with pictures or in other creative ways. What you want is for it to be memorized.

That is what this section is for: so that they can do this intellectual exercise and assimilate in their hearts the meaning and implications of the phrase that is presented to them in each lesson.

In this case you can ask them some questions like:

- What does this phrase mean to you?

- In what ways should we be like Jesus?

- What are his best qualities?

- What things did Jesus do that you still don't do?

NOTE: If you have already asked each boy and girl to have a notebook or journal ready to be their DISCIPLE'S JOURNAL, tell them to write this sentence very big there.

 # REFLECT ON A CHARACTER

Remember that you can choose both characters or just one of them as an example for the theme. The decision will depend on how much time you have for the meeting and how deep you want to go into each proposed character.

You can read the text here or be inspired by it to tell the story. Use photographs, papers, or a projector with images. That always helps! You can also use costumes or masks to play the character as you tell your story.

BATMAN, ROBIN, AND BATGIRL

He wears a dark suit and has bat ears on his hood. But what does Batman do? He keeps an eye on Gotham City so that none of the villains of the city do their evil deeds. But it is not easy to keep watch over a city so big and with so many problems without having help, and although Batman never asked for it, destiny gave him an ally, an adventure companion, a disciple to teach what a hero needs to know to do justice.

So along came Robin. He is Batman's apprentice. In this way, Batman has someone to teach everything he knows, and Robin has a teacher from whom he can learn everything. The young disciple is often wrong, but Batman is there to put him back on the right path.

And with Batgirl the same thing happens. She arrives unannounced and joins the team. She has many qualities of her own, and she is brave just like the other two, but she is also aware of who is leading and knows that she must learn to follow.

In addition, there is another issue that is worth highlighting. Batman is the leader, brave and cunning, but from time to time, in difficult moments, even he has to ask someone like Alfred, his elderly butler, who has the wisdom that the years bring, for help.

QUESTIONS FOR YOUR DISCIPLES:

- What is Robin to Batman? And Batgirl?

- Do you know of any other examples of superheroes with disciples?

- What would Robin and Batgirl have to imitate Batman?

As you talk about the characters and ask the questions, it is good that you can get interaction with your boys and girls. Ask them, for example, to raise their hand if they would choose to be like Batman, or like Robin and Batgirl, that is, if they prefer to teach or learn.

Before you finish, be sure to tell them that as Jesus's disciples, we are all going to learn from him, and we are also going to teach others what we have learned.

JOHN

They say that he was the youngest disciple of Jesus. It is said that he was so close to the teacher that when they were resting, John would rest his head on Jesus's chest. They were close friends, yes, but John never stopped being his disciple. And although John was not the one who walked on water, nor was he one of those who fought to be in a privileged place in heaven, he was the one who received the greatest secrets about the kingdom of heaven.

The gospel that John wrote is called "the gospel of love" and there John calls himself "the beloved disciple." He also received revelation about very deep spiritual things in the book of Revelation and was able to write some letters to the Christian communities of that time.

John walked with Jesus from the beginning of his earthly ministry, and he never stopped being a disciple. He remained a disciple even when he was very, very old.

QUESTIONS FOR YOUR DISCIPLES:

- What things make John a good disciple?

- What areas of John's life can we imitate?

 # MOBILIZE

This is a good time to pull out the journal. If you haven't written the memory phrase yet, now is a good time to do so and you'll also add a memory verse:

As the Father has loved me, so have I loved you. Now remain in my love.
(John 15:9)

Show them that verse in a big way, give them copies and you can write it on a poster and cover different words at a time to have them memorize it little by little.

Remember that in order to achieve in-depth work with the children, you must be in contact with their parents to coordinate, for example, activities like this. It is not a matter of placing a burden on them that they cannot carry, that can be overwhelming, or that takes up too much time. The purpose is to keep in mind the spiritual goal of the week as something concrete to work on as they grow as disciples, so give parents the phrase and verse to repeat with their kids at home.

Look at the following chart (we'll tell you what to do with it below). Here we return to the qualities of Jesus that we saw earlier in the lesson, and for each quality an example of personal application is listed. In other words, the second column answers the question: What could I do to be like Jesus in this regard?

HOW WAS JESUS?	MY GOAL OF THE WEEK
He loved people.	Demonstrate love or affection to someone.
He was compassionate.	Give an offering to someone in need.
He was gentle and humble.	Act with patience and without pride.
He was obedient to his Father.	Be obedient to my parents.
He was honest.	Always tell the truth.
He prayed all the time.	Look for someone to pray with every day.
He denounced evil.	Tell my parents if I see something that is wrong or unjust.
He served others.	Do at least one act of service for someone.
He knew the Word of God well.	Memorize one Bible verse this week.
He gave hope.	Cheer up someone who is feeling low.

INSTRUCTIONS

- Make a copy of this chart for each disciple in your group. You can photocopy it or take a photo of the page in this book and print as many copies as you need. Also, if you want to make it more elaborate, you can design your own picture frame.

- Ask them to choose a page from the DISCIPLE'S JOURNAL and place the heading "LESSON 1: WHO IS A DISCIPLE?"

- Ask them to glue the table that you have previously prepared for them there.

- Then have them each choose one of Jesus's qualities to make that their personal goal for the week. If they choose obedience, for example, then they must demonstrate that quality throughout the week. They can underline or color the chosen word so they don't forget it.

Have them take home the key phrase of the lesson not only in the journal but give them some kind of card or bookmark with it.

The more I look like Jesus, the better disciple I become.

Before finishing, explain to them that during the week they can record their progress in the journal with writing or drawing. Emphasize that this notebook is personal to each one, since it will be like their "travel journal" and in it they will write down the path they travel on this journey.

At the end of the lesson, pray for each boy and girl in your group, so that they yearn to become more like Jesus every day and can take concrete steps to move toward that goal. (If you can say each of their names in your prayer that's better, and if there are too many, divide them into smaller groups and use your volunteers to do this.)

THE BIBLE IS AN ADVENTURE

The Bible is not man´s word about God, but God's word about man.

John Barth

Just as Alice was able to enter Wonderland, a fantastic world full of color and the most impressive things, we too can enter a supernatural world through the Bible. It's crazy that some say they don't like to read the Bible! Of course, to understand it, mere intelligence is not enough. It takes imagination.

God, the creator of the universe, decided to capture in the Holy Scriptures everything that could help us live in a supernatural way in this natural world. The Bible is an adventure! A trip to the past, present, and future. A date with characters who could experience events that would not have occurred to even the best of writers.

What madness! To say that the Bible is just a book full of history is to miss out on the wealth it contains!

Therefore, in this lesson we will help our boys and girls to look beyond what natural eyes can see. It is essential that they become passionate about the Word of God from an early age, so that they become not only heirs of a religion, but bearers of the life that the Word offers!

IT IS ESSENTIAL THAT THEY BECOME PASSIONATE ABOUT THE WORD OF GOD FROM AN EARLY AGE, SO THAT THEY BECOME NOT ONLY HEIRS OF A RELIGION, BUT BEARERS OF THE LIFE THAT THE WORD OFFERS!

Sooner or later our boys and girls will be exposed to the popular thought that what the Bible says is not true, God does not exist, and all that this book contains are fables that are useless in real life. So this lesson is vital to inject passion, imagination, and certainty into the hearts of those little ones who are learning from you.

Let's do this!

 AVALANCHE OF IDEAS

ACTIVITY: ADVENTURE CONTEST

Divide your children into three small groups and assign each group one of the adventures to re-create:

1. Alice in Wonderland

2. The Chronicles of Narnia

3. The Jungle Book

These are three books that have been brought to the big screen. In order to carry out this activity you must obtain enough materials so that all the children can participate. What are they going to do? They're going to create!

Some ideas for materials you can use are: fabric scraps, newspaper, masking tape, plastic, thick and thin string, a few sticks of glue, and anything else you can think of to awaken the creativity of the children.

Each of the teams must re-create a character from the story that was assigned to the group. Here are some examples of characters:

1. Alice in Wonderland

    a. The mad hatter

    b. The white rabbit

    c. Alice

2. The Chronicles of Narnia

    a. Lucy, who found the door to Narnia

    b. Jadis, the white witch

    c. The lion

3. The Jungle Book

    a. Mowgli, the boy from the jungle

    b. Shere Khan, the tiger

    c. Kaa, the manipulative snake

One of the children in the group should serve as a model and the others will build the costume on the boy or girl who has been chosen as a model.

When the costumes are ready, give them instructions on how to introduce themselves to the rest, or have someone from each group introduce their model. They could also act out a scene from the movie saying a couple of phrases that they remember. It all depends on how much time you have for the whole lesson. In any case, this activity should not last more than 15 minutes.

CONDITIONS

- They have a time limit of 10 minutes to prepare the costumes.

- There will be a prize for the best costume.

- There will be a prize for the best performance.

- There will be a prize for whoever does it the fastest.

We want children to learn to compete healthily. That is why you must prepare three prizes. One will be for each group, and thus everyone will win in one of the categories and no one will have lost.

Also consider that if the children are younger, they may need more time and help from you. If they are older, you can increase the difficulty.

On the other hand, if your group is not large enough, you can divide it into 2 groups instead of three and choose two of the three movies to work on.

FOUNDATIONS OF THE THEME

The Bible is an exciting adventure, not only for children but for young and old alike! And it is really a privilege for each disciple to be able to be part of that adventure.

Tell the group that in the Bible we can find many different types of stories (you can use pictures or project images to illustrate each item). There we find...

- Great battles.

- Supernatural encounters.

- Feats and wonders.

- Adventures in the sea, forest, and cities.

- Prisoners who were released.

- And many more stories!

(If you wish, you can enlarge the list by including brothers who quarreled, or stories of betrayal and faithfulness, among others. In fact, if we were to put together a list of all the adventures found in the Word of God, it would be a very long list!)

The most interesting thing is that what is described there is true. They are not fables or legends. Excluding some parables, the vast majority are true stories with characters who really existed, and with eyewitnesses to each of the stories that are told there.

The Bible is the best-selling book of all time, and although many have tried to distort it, no one has yet been able to prove that the Bible is not true. On the contrary, more and more scientists and historians are coming to the conclusion that the Bible is completely accurate and is itself a miracle.

> **IF WE WERE TO PUT TOGETHER A LIST OF ALL THE ADVENTURES FOUND IN THE WORD OF GOD, IT WOULD BE A VERY LONG LIST!**

When you look at it from that perspective, you get even more excited, because you remember that you are talking to your boys and girls about real stories. People who spoke in strange languages that they did not know, someone who was able to stop the rain for 3 years and then call it back, another who stopped the rotation of the Earth for a whole day, and many more who prophesied things that were coming true one by one. We are not talking about just any book, but about the true life of God hidden in words!

Can that be boring?

Never!

Read in one sitting, it can be enjoyed as an extraordinarily well-written novel, full of special effects and mind-blowing situations. When you finish reading Revelation you feel inspired, challenged to live out your faith in a real way, through examples that are very striking and delve deep into your being.

Alex Sampedro *(Artesano) [Craftsman]*

Just like when you watch a movie and identify with the characters and imagine being there in the scene, the same thing happens with the Word of God. Each story speaks to our hearts. They are experiences of others that God uses so that we experience his truth in the different situations that we must face every day.

Also, the Bible never hides anything. It tells you things as they happened. It doesn't need to pretend that something didn't happen, it doesn't seek to enlarge an already enormous feat, nor does it try to minimize the mistakes and falls of those characters we admire. That's why we know that everything in the Bible is real!

"Looking closely, people wonder why the stories in the Bible are so con-
flicted, difficult, and even violent. It's honestly something to be grateful for.
It means that God is really involved in our world, not an imaginary world;
God is writing a story in real lives, in real time, and in a real way.
Reggie Joiner and Lucas Leys (Los padres que tus hijos necesitan)
[The parents that your children need]

📖 FOCUS ON TRUTH

Now we are going to take the list from the previous section, and we will give an example of a biblical story for each case.

- Great battles

  ◊ Joshua 6

    - The Israelites tear down a great wall with screams and trumpets, and thus they can take the city of Jericho.

- Supernatural encounters.

  ◊ Genesis 32:22-30

    - Jacob has an encounter with the angel of Jehovah and even wrestles with him to ask for his blessing.

- Feats and wonders

    ◊ 1 Kings 17:1; 1 Kings 18:42-45

        ▪ Elijah orders the rain to stop and then prays for it to rain again.

- Adventures in the sea, forest, and cities

    ◊ Jonah 1

        ▪ Jonah refuses to give a message from God to the city of Nineveh and tries to flee in a boat, but a great storm comes, and he is thrown into the sea, where he is swallowed by a great fish. He spends three days inside the fish until he repents and cries out to the Lord, and then the Lord makes the fish vomit him up on the beach.

- Prisoners who were released.

    ◊ Acts 12:1-11

        ▪ Peter is visited by an angel of God who miraculously frees him from prison.

You can tell your children something like the following:

"The Bible is full of adventures waiting to be discovered by those who decide to embark on that journey!"

Next, you will take one of those adventures to tell the children in the form of a story. But don't just tell them the story. Ask them to act as if they were in it, to imitate the gestures, the sensations... to live the adventure!

We find this story in Exodus 15:22-27...

A few days had passed since God parted the Red Sea so the Israelites could cross over and escape the Egyptians, but now they were in the desert.

What is it like to be in the desert?

There is nowhere to find food or water and walking under the desert sun can be very exhausting. During the day it is too hot, and at night it is too cold.

The Israelites needed water! Where could there be water?

Deserts are famous for not having water for many, many miles. This is how the Israelites had to travel, by foot, for many miles looking for water.

(You can have the children walk around the room as if they are exhausted and thirsty.)

After spending 3 days looking for water, they finally reached Mara, a place where there was water, but when they drank from it. . . yuk! It was bitter water, undrinkable!

(Have them pretend to taste bitter water.)

Many complained against God and against Moses, asking why they had been taken to the desert to die of thirst. But once again, God used Moses to perform a miracle.

(You can ask one of the children to play the role of Moses.)

So, Moses walked following God's instructions, took a tree trunk, and threw it into those waters and suddenly, without anyone expecting it, boom! The waters became sweet, and all the people could drink of it.

(Give the children some water right now. Let them feel how sweet the water God sends can be.)

Then ask the group: What can we learn from this story?

Let the children tell you their own conclusions, but also think of some ideas you may have ready to guide them, such as:

- God does miracles all the time.

- We should not complain but ask God for what we need.

- Our life can be dry and sad, bitter. But God can change that sadness and bitterness into joy. He always sends us the waters of life so that we feel that way.

Have you realized yet, every Bible story can be lived as an adventure!

 INTROSPECTION

Remember that this space is intended for children to reflect on the chosen phrase, and not just learn it by heart. Learning the phrase is good, but what we want is for children to think for themselves about their faith, to reason with it, and for it not to be a set of rules that they repeat to themselves. Especially since that stops making sense when they hit their preteens!

The phrase for this lesson is:

I am part of the story of the Bible.

To help them reflect on the phrase, encourage them to answer some questions:

- Why do we say that the Bible is an adventure?

- How can I be a part of the Bible adventure every day?

 REFLECT ON A CHARACTER

This part of the lesson tries to lead the children to find a reference that helps them remember or illustrate what we are teaching them. Rather than telling or reading to them what is written here, the ideal would be to create a conversation with the children. Some may not know the character. That's why it's good that during the week you talk to their parents and ask them if they know the character. You can also encourage parents to talk about the character during the week before the lesson, so that the children will arrive ready.

MULAN

The mountains were difficult terrain in which to engage the enemy, and it was there that the Chinese warriors encountered the Hunnic army. Those barbarians were huge, they had formidable swords and spears, and their bodies seemed to be twice the size of Mulan.

For their part, the warriors of the Chinese army were inexperienced in battle, and their captain was very young as well. The battle ahead was impossible to win.

The first blows left Mulan and her friends ready to surrender, which was the most logical thing to do. Suddenly, an idea crossed the mind of the impromptu young warrior: she would take a cannon and launch it just before Shan Yu, the ruthless leader of the Huns, reached them.

The cannon grazed the barbarian's head, and he taunted Mulan thinking that she had missed. But it was not like that. The cannon landed right on the top of the mountain, causing an avalanche of snow to completely cover their enemies. Mulan and her friends were jumping for joy. Everyone congratulated Mulan for such an enormous feat. They still thought Mulan was a boy, but they were about to find out the truth.

QUESTIONS FOR YOUR DISCIPLES:

- What positive attitudes can we highlight in Mulan?

- Would you dare to live an adventure like this? Why or why not?

- How is this adventure like the Bible?

JONAH

The story of Jonah is one of the most told stories in the Bible. He was a prophet who did not want to obey God's command to alert the city of Nineveh to repent. To flee, Jonah went on a boat trip, and being on the high seas, a storm was about to wreck the ship. Soon the occupants of the boat realized that this storm had come because of Jonah, so they decided to throw him into the water. It was then that a large fish appeared and swallowed him whole.

Can you imagine how big that fish would have been to swallow a whole person?

For three days Jonah was inside the animal, until he finally repented. And just at the moment when he decided to obey God, the fish vomited him out of its belly and threw him onto the shore.

QUESTIONS FOR YOUR DISCIPLES:

- Would you dare to disobey an order from God? Why or why not?

- Would you jump into an adventure even knowing that it could go very wrong for you? Why or why not?

- How are you like Jonah?

MOBILIZE

Let's work on the DISCIPLE'S JOURNAL!

Ask the children under the heading "Lesson 2" to write the following sentence:

I am part of the story of the Bible.

For this week, ask each child to choose a biblical adventure they would've liked to have been a part of. Then they choose to be one of the characters, and they can tell that story as if they had been participating.

YOU CAN GUIDE THEM WITH THE FOLLOWING QUESTIONS:

- What is the biblical story that you would have liked to live?

- What character in that story would you have liked to be?

- Why did you choose that character?

- How are you like him or her?

In their journals they can write the whole story, or just the answers to the questions. They can also draw pictures to illustrate the story.

This is an activity they can get their parents involved in! In fact, they will be the first to hear the story, and it would be good if the children could work with the help of their parents.

Of course, don't forget that when you start the meeting the following week you should ask them how it went, read their stories, and congratulate them on their work!

Before the meeting ends, pray that each of the boys and girls in your group will always yearn to be a part of the exciting adventure of the Bible.

LESSON 3

MY RELATIONSHIP WITH GOD

*Always, everywhere God is present, and always He seeks
to discover Himself to each one.*

A.W. Tozer

Being in a relationship with someone involves connecting with another person. One can meet many people but without being friends or really connecting. Today technology can help us connect with people, but with or without technology, a relationship has to do with two people who get to know each other more and more, and the same thing happens with God.

It is one thing to know that this person exists, and another to talk to them. It is one thing to know that you have an uncle named Carlos and another to have a relationship with uncle Carlos. It is one thing to admit that God exists and another to begin to connect and relate to Him.

 AVALANCHE OF IDEAS

ACTIVITY: WHO IS THIS PERSON?

Get pictures of your children's parents. You can show them with a projector or print them on paper. If you have a virtual meeting, it will be easy to show the photos by sharing the screen or you can also do it on a tablet and show the photos live.

To start the meeting, tell them that you are going to show them photos of very important people and that the children must identify who each one is. You can have a short description of each person ready as if they were someone famous.

For example:

"This man is a great worker. He is the most important salesperson in his company. He has many friends, and they all like him. The most important person in his life is his wife."

Do this for all the parents you show. When you do, obviously a boy or girl in the group will jump up saying that it is their mom or dad. When that happens, you should look shocked. Wow! This important character is now part of our lesson.

When the boy or girl identifies their father or mother, ask them to tell everyone what they like most about him or her. So they don't forget, write their answers on a board. At the end of the activity, remind them what each one said about their mom or dad, and ask for a round of applause for everyone.

Tell them clearly that today's topic is "My relationship with God."

FOUNDATIONS OF THE THEME

We were created to connect with one another, and the way this happens on a human level is also essential when it comes to our relationship with God.

> *"God has created us for authentic connection and meaningful attach-ment—the kind of connection that has the power to give us security, growth, freedom, and transformation."*
> **Archibald Hart (Digital Invasion)**

And so, if being connected with other people is so necessary to us, imagine how much more important our connection with the Creator of the universe is!

Believing in God is not enough. According to Scripture even the demons believe in him and are afraid of him. That is why the fact of believing is not enough. Getting closer to God is like a path in which we are advancing little by little. Just like it happens with a person you barely know, as you spend time together, you get to know each other better. That's what a relationship is all about!

Explain to the children that our faith is incomplete if there is not an intimate relationship with God.

IF BEING CONNECTED WITH OTHER PEOPLE IS SO NECESSARY TO US, IMAGINE HOW MUCH MORE IMPORTANT OUR CONNECTION WITH THE CREATOR OF THE UNIVERSE IS!

The way they connect with a friend, with a teacher, or with their parents is key to understanding how their relationship with God will work.

Have the children reflect on how this process works by showing them the following example about how they come to make a new friend:

At first, someone tells you about a new friend, or introduces them to you. You like that person, and you decide to look for moments to interact more. There is still no connection at this stage; you just spend time together, get to know each other more, and start to see what you have in common. If you continue to encourage the friendship, soon you will find more personal moments, ways to help each other, and you will start to learn to resolve your conflicts. If all that goes well, after a while you will have learned to stay connected to each other, and you will be able to enjoy a friendly relationship. If that connection doesn't work out well, the relationship will remain fleeting, like memories of someone you once knew.

To connect with God we must also go through some stages. These could be summarized in the following table, which we will call STAGES IN MY PERSONAL RELATIONSHIP WITH GOD. This table is similar to another that we have included in the books for preteens and teens, but here we have adapted it so that it is more understandable for the little ones.

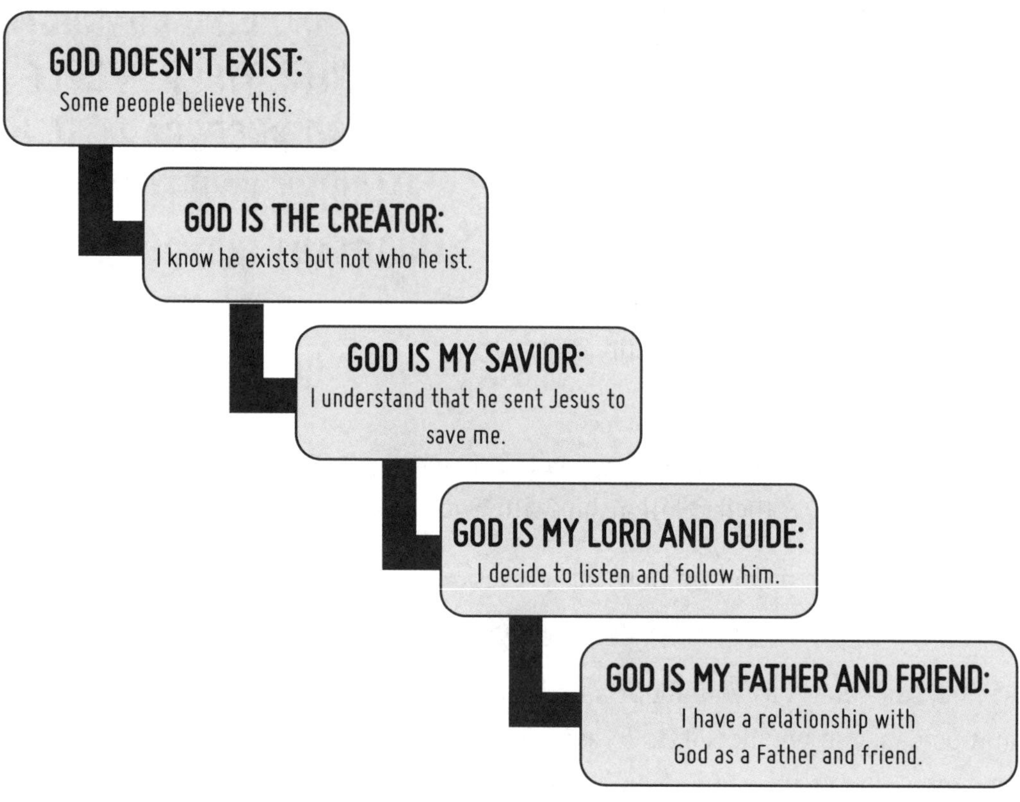

What does a person think and feel at each level?

1. GOD DOESN'T EXIST:

   ◊   This is the position of the atheist.

   ◊   Have never had real contact with God.

   ◊   There is no connection or relationship with him.

2. GOD IS THE CREATOR:

   ◊   Believe that God created all things.

   ◊   They cannot find any purpose to his existence.

⬧ There is no connection or relationship with him.

3. GOD IS MY SAVIOR:

   ⬧ Understands that only God can save and has accepted that salvation.

   ⬧ Starts to pray, although still doesn't know how.

   ⬧ Feels a desire to have a connection with him.

4. GOD IS MY LORD AND GUIDE:

   ⬧ Understands that God is King, and his Word should be obeyed.

   ⬧ Starts to connect with the truth about him through prayer and reading his Word.

   ⬧ Is his disciple and obeys his Word.

5. GOD IS MY FATHER AND FRIEND:

   ⬧ Relates to God as a Father and friend.

   ⬧ Looks to build that relationship every day.

   ⬧ Is a disciple who teaches others to have a relationship with God.

The goal for the disciples is to get to number five and stay there.

📖 FOCUS ON TRUTH

There is no better example in the Bible than that of Jesus. Always connected with the Father, always praying in the early mornings, not out of habit or obligation but out of necessity. Always looking to the Father before making important decisions at crucial moments. From his childhood to his last breath of natural

THERE IS NO BETTER EXAMPLE IN THE BIBLE THAN THAT OF JESUS.

life, he did everything to please God without taking away the glory that only belongs to him.

Where do we notice Jesus's connection to the Father?

- In his prayers: There we can see his longing to be alone with the Father.

- In his speeches: He always used the Word of God to speak with people.

- In his miracles: When he performed a miracle, Jesus gave glory to the Father.

- When he talked about anything and shared life with his disciples: At all times his words and actions denoted an intimate relationship with God.

- In his way of living: There was no sin in him, since he always knew that he was set apart for God, which means he was holy. For this reason, Jesus himself asks us to be holy, set apart for God, and always connected with our Father, in all circumstances, through all calamities, and with all blessings.

LET'S DO IT!

Prepare four stations in your meeting place. Each should have an item that the children can identify so they never forget this portion of the lesson. The stations are for the four moments that will be described. Here is a suggestion of how you can build each station:

For Jesus's baptism: Place a container full of water, bring a doll that represents Jesus, and get a toy dove.

For Jesus's preteen years. Get a toy house that represents the temple where Jesus was teaching.

For Jesus with his disciples: You can use a toy boat and a net to fish. With that you can represent when Jesus called Peter and he left his nets to follow him.

For prayer: Get a picture or drawing that represents Jesus raising his hands to pray. This was evidence that he was always seeking the Father.

As you take the children through each station, let them experiment with each one. Don't mind if they play a little with the water, or if they drop something on the floor. They are children, and it is necessary that they enjoy while they learn!

Tell each story passionately, and do not forget that in each one there is a reference to the relationship of Jesus with his Father. Emphasize that

Here you have the four stories:

- At his baptism, before beginning his public ministry...

"When all the people were being baptized, Jesus was baptized too. And as he was praying, heaven was opened and the Holy Spirit descended on him in bodily form like a dove. And a voice came from heaven: "You are my Son, whom I love; with you I am well pleased."
(Luke 3:21-22)

...the Father's words affirmed the connection between the two.

- When he was a preteen, at 12 years old...

"Why were you searching for me?" he asked. "Didn't you know I had to be in my Father's house?"
(Luke 2:49)

...Jesus was certain that the Father wanted him there, doing his Father's work.

- In the choice of his disciples...

One of those days Jesus went out to a mountainside to pray, and spent the night praying to God. When morning came, he called his disciples to him and chose twelve of them, whom he also designated apostles: Simon (whom he named Peter), his brother Andrew, James, John, Philip,

Bartholomew, Matthew, Thomas, James son of Alphaeus, Simon who was called the Zealot, Judas son of James, and Judas Iscariot, who became a traitor.
(Luke 6:12-16)

...who spent all night praying? Jesus.

- When he taught them to pray...

He said to them, "When you pray, say: 'Father, hallowed be your name, your kingdom come. Give us each day our daily bread. Forgive us our sins, for we also forgive everyone who sins against us. And lead us not into temptation."
(Luke 11:2-4)

...the Father was always in his prayers.

⚙ INTROSPECTION

Have all the children write in the DISCIPLE'S JOURNAL the key phrase of today's lesson:

My relationship with God is more important than everything else.

Then come the reflection questions:

- Who is more important, God or my parents? Why?

- Are my friends more important than God? Why or why not?

- How do I know if I have a good relationship with God?

- What can I do to grow in my relationship with God?

Make sure that all the boys and girls participate in all the sections, and when there are questions, like there are here, allow them to say everything they think. Our role as disciplers is not to tell children what to believe but to help them think for themselves.

 REFLECT ON A CHARACTER

LUCY

C. S. Lewis is the author of the seven book series, *The Chronicles of Narnia*. In the book entitled *The Lion, the Witch and the Wardrobe* we meet four siblings. The youngest of them is Lucy. Little Lucy is the one who finds the entrance door to the fantastic world of Narnia for the first time, and that is the beginning of a great adventure.

We will talk about Lucy because it is precisely she who is connected for the first time with the world of Narnia, but also because she is the one who is most connected to the lion Aslan, the creator of everything, and ruler of Narnia. Lucy's relationship with Aslan was very special from the beginning, both on the part of the girl (who marveled at the enormity of the majestic lion), and on the part of Aslan (who felt great tenderness and special affection for the innocent Lucy).

We know that Aslan represents the lion of the tribe of Judah, that is, Jesus. And Lucy is a figure of all of us, those of us who seek God and want to feel protected by him.

Lucy presents us with the need to connect with God in an intimate, constant, and permanent way. That connection is something we should never lack!

QUESTIONS FOR YOUR DISCIPLES:

- Do you feel connected or disconnected with God? Why?

- When have you felt that God has been protecting you?

- Do you feel that God is speaking to you? How does he do it?

SAMUEL

Samuel was a little boy who served in the temple. One night, while he was resting, he heard a voice calling him and he thought it was Eli the priest.

—Samuel, Samuel —the voice repeated, incessantly.

—What do you want, Eli? —Samuel answered, going to where the priest was, since he thought that was who was calling him.

— It wasn't me who called you—answered the priest—go back to sleep.

This happened over and over again, until Eli understood that Samuel was listening to the voice of God and he was able to instruct the boy so that he would learn to respond when God called him.

Thanks to the fact that Samuel was attentive to the voice of God from a young age, he later became one of the most important prophets in the history of Israel. He was the one who anointed Saul as king, and then the famous David as well!

QUESTIONS FOR YOUR DISCIPLES:

- Have you ever heard the voice of God? How was it, and under what circumstances?

- What are you doing, or what do you think you could do, to connect with him?

 # MOBILIZE

ACTIVITY: MATCH THE ANSWERS

Photocopy or take a picture of the chart below and print it ahead of time so the boys and girls can glue it in their journals. You can also ask them to copy it from a board.

MATCH THE ANSWERS	
WITH THIS PERSON:	**MY RELATIONSHIP SHOULD BE:**
God	Respectful
My parents	Affectionate
My siblings	Intimate
My teachers	Trustworthy
My leaders	Loving
My pet	Faithful

Talk to each other about how each one solved the activity. At some point in the exercise the children will realize that most adjectives can fit well with different people. For example, we can have a trustworthy or affectionate relationship with God, although ideally it would be intimate.

The purpose of this activity is for boys and girls to identify God as the most important relationship of all. In fact, the relationship with God should be respectful, affectionate, intimate, trustworthy, loving, and faithful! Therefore, with God, all the answers are correct! However, you cannot have an intimate or respectful relationship with a pet. It's good for the kids to be able to identify that difference!

It is probable that some say that they see God only with respect, and that their connection goes no further. You should encourage them to improve that connection more and more, since one of the hallmarks of discipleship is growing in our relationship with God!

If the parents of the children in your group are Christians, take this opportunity to talk with them, tell them your purposes throughout this process of discipleship, and tell them how they can help you. For example, you can ask them to tell their children during the week how they have grown in their relationship with God since they met him until now, how they have felt his presence, and how they have heard his voice.

Before ending the meeting, give them a card or bookmark with the prayer known as "The Lord's Prayer" from Matthew 6:9-13 and recommend that they memorize it even with some final game. And lastly, do not forget to ask the children to write down in their DISCIPLE'S JOURNAL the phrase of the week:

My relationship with God is more important than everything else.

Pray for this phrase to come true in the life of each boy and girl in your group!

THE KINGDOM OF HEAVEN

The only way the kingdom of God is going to be manifest in this world before Christ comes is if we manifest it by the way we live as citizens of heaven and subjects of the King.

R. C. Sproul

C. S. Lewis was one of the most renowned apologists of the last century. His theological writings show his firm convictions about Christ but in the literary field, Lewis impacted the world through *The Chronicles of Narnia*, a series of seven books that present a fantastic world that, for someone who knows the gospel thoroughly, illustrates the story of redemption.

Narnia is a kingdom of peace that has been subdued by the white witch to make it a cold and evil place. In the same way, our world has been invaded by Satan and his spiritual hosts of evil. Aslan, which in Turkish means lion, is the ruler of all Narnia, just as Jesus, the lion of Judah, is our King and Lord.

Whether we are aware of it or not, the truth is that we all move in a spiritual reality. Day by day we live in the middle of a battle between two kingdoms, although sometimes we don't even notice it. The empire of darkness is real, and we must work to establish the kingdom of heaven in every corner of this world. But first it must be established in our hearts.

AVALANCHE OF IDEAS

ACTIVITY: IMITATE THE KING

Materials:

- A crown (this can be one you bought as part of a costume, but it will also work if you make it yourself out of cardboard or paper)

- A die (it can be a small one of those that come in board games, or you could build a giant one to make it look more impressive)

Instructions:

Arrange all the children in a circle. To show them what to do, start by putting the crown on your head. Then do a movement that the children can repeat (for example, jump and clap your hands once). Everyone must shout "Imitate the King, Imitate the King!" and at the same time they will have to carry out the action you have proposed.

When everyone has understood what they should do, roll the die, and according to the number that comes up, count the children to your right. The one whose turn it is will receive the crown and must make a movement for everyone to imitate. Remind them that they cannot repeat the action that someone else has already done. And don't forget that everyone must shout the phrase "Imitate the king!" while they do it.

Ideally, this game would last until all or most of the children have been able to be king, but also do not extend the activity so long that they get bored. It is better to stop it when they are still having fun, and if the children want to play a little more, you can repeat the activity at the end of the meeting or next week.

 FOUNDATIONS OF THE THEME

Jesus came to preach the good news of the gospel of the kingdom of heaven. He himself declared that the kingdom had already drawn near thanks to his coming.

For a long time, it was thought that the kingdom of heaven was a place where we will all live in the future when we are no longer in this world. Now, we understand that it is not only a place we will go one day, but it is an active kingdom that manifests itself today in our midst.

As is the case in every kingdom, there is a king, and that king is Jesus. In the Gospels, several times we find Jesus giving instructions on how to live on this earth to manifest the truths of his kingdom. Most of the times that Jesus spoke about this subject, he did it through parables: stories to illustrate how that kingdom works among us.

And the funny thing is... it works the opposite way of what we're used to! Teach your children the following truths about the kingdom of heaven:

- **The last will be first and the first will be last.** The one who is desperate to enter, can enter last.

- **To be big you must be the smallest.** It is not necessary to look for greatness but humility.

- **The one who is above all is the one who serves all.** Leaders must be willing to serve others.

- **Children have a special place.** Children's hearts allow them to see the kingdom of heaven.

- **It is not a kingdom for the rich but for the poor in spirit.** The one who seeks earthly riches cannot easily attain eternal things.

- **It is not visible to all but only to the pure in heart.** It is necessary to purify our hearts to see the wonders of God.

- **Treasures are not money or precious stones.** God has prepared immense treasures for us, but not like those of this world.

- **Everything moves through faith.** Sometimes reason cannot explain what happens in the kingdom of heaven, as is the case with miracles and healings.

"Undoubtedly, Jesus, who knew children very well, saw in them expectation, amazement, surprise, confidence, and humility... and these are characteristics that the Lord looks for in the lives of people of any age so that they may receive the kingdom of God".
Jessica Ibarbalz *(Manual de consejería para el trabajo con niños)*
[Counseling Manual for children's work]

CHILDREN HAVE AN OPEN DOOR TO THE KINGDOM OF HEAVEN AND THAT DOOR IS JESUS.

Jesus often uses the image of a door or gate referring to a path on which we must travel. Children have an open door to the kingdom of heaven and that door is Jesus. This means that knowing and following Jesus opens the doors to this supernatural world of God and his kingdom.

How do I get closer to the kingdom of heaven?

Share these answers with your children:

- Draw near to God, believing that he exists and that he can show you the wonders of his kingdom today.

- Seek to get to know the king, who is Jesus, more each day.

- Don't do things out of habit. Seek God genuinely and sincerely.

- Guard your heart and do not let it be contaminated with unbelief.

📖 FOCUS ON TRUTH

In this section we will look at the parable of the hidden treasure and the valuable pearl. This is one of the many parables that Jesus told about the kingdom of heaven, and it goes like this:

"The kingdom of heaven is like treasure hidden in a field. When a man found it, he hid it again, and then in his joy went and sold all he had and bought that field.
Again, the kingdom of heaven is like a merchant looking for fine pearls. When he found one of great value, he went away and sold everything he had and bought it"
(Matthew 13:44-46)

Some things we can learn from this parable are:

- The kingdom of heaven is a treasure with infinite value.

- The kingdom of heaven is hard to find; it is hidden.

- Finding it fills us with joy.

LET'S PLAY HIDDEN TREASURE!

According to the number of participants you have, prepare posters with the word "Jesus" and hide them (before the meeting) in different places in the room. If you prefer, you can use pearls instead, or both.

Of course, keep in mind the ages of the children, since for some it will be easier to find the treasure than others. The important thing is that there is a poster or a pearl for each boy or girl. That is, no one can be left without that treasure.

As they find it, ask each child what they would be willing to give up in exchange for that treasure. The parable says that those who found the treasure and the pearl sold everything they had in order to keep them!

QUESTIONS FOR THE CHILDREN:

- What does it mean when someone sells everything to keep the treasure?

- How valuable is it for you to know Jesus?

INTROSPECTION

The phrase that we want the children to remember from this lesson is:

Jesus is worth more than any treasure.

Why? Because it's only when we put Jesus first in our lives that all the other kingdom values fall into place.

Jesus himself said:

But seek first his kingdom and his righteousness, and all these things will be given to you as well.
(Matthew 6:33)

HELP THE CHILDREN REFLECT WITH A FEW QUESTIONS:

- What things on earth can be a treasure?

- Is your faith in Jesus more important than everything? Why or why not?

- What would you do if someone asked you to leave Jesus in exchange for a lot of money?

REFLECT ON A CHARACTER

Remember that for this space you can use pictures, but you can also show them a video with an excerpt from the film. That will be very attractive to children! Just be careful not to take too much time for this. two or three minutes will suffice.

SIMBA

Mufasa has just had a son, who will be the heir and ruler of the entire savannah when his time comes. Simba. That was the name of the lion cub. Mammals, birds, reptiles all surrender to the king of the jungle, the lion king.

Scar, Mufasa's brother, is not very fond of this idea. He plans the king's death and blames Simba for it. The cub is then forced to flee his home and, full of fear, and leaves the savannah, his own kingdom, behind.

As a child, Simba was a cocky cub, proud, and confident in the fact that he was a prince. Running away, he learned to be a carefree slacker, unable to face problems. Years passed before Simba realized the importance of facing the past and correcting his mistakes.

Looking back on his life, Simba must face his grief over the loss of his father, but upon learning that his kingdom is in danger, he decides to go back and make things right with his uncle face-to-face. Simba is no longer the smug cub he used to be. He is now a humble lion and has grown wiser. Thanks to these qualities, he manages to defeat the evil Scar and is recognized again as the lion king.

QUESTIONS FOR YOUR DISCIPLES:

- Have you ever run from problems like Simba did? If so, when?

- What does it mean to be conceited?

- What do you think you should do to be a good heir to the kingdom of heaven?

THOMAS

Thomas is probably the most criticized disciple of Jesus in all of history. Despite having been one of the twelve disciples whom Jesus taught, and, having heard about the promise of the resurrection of Jesus, when the time came Thomas doubted that the one he was seeing was his resurrected teacher.

Jesus told Thomas to put his finger in the hollow of his hand, just where the thick nails, with which they had crucified him, had passed. Thomas did so, and only then was he convinced that this was really Jesus. At the moment that this happened, Thomas said to Jesus: "My Lord and my God!"

There are definitely times when we are all like Thomas. We doubt something and Jesus gives us the ability to trust him even more and realize that he is always our main treasure.

QUESTIONS FOR YOUR DISCIPLES:

- Why would Thomas have doubted when he saw Jesus come back from the dead?

- If you saw the risen Jesus, would you have doubted that it was him? Why or why not?

MOBILIZE

Look for a drawing that the kids can color of the lion king, or Aslan or, if you prefer, any image that represents the lion of the tribe of Judah, that is, Jesus in the form of a Lion.

Ask them to color it and stick it in their journals. Then tell them that during the week they should use that image to share with someone else what they have learned about the kingdom of heaven. Keep in mind that the best learning is the one that occurs when we teach others what we learned!

Who should they tell? It can be to their parents or siblings, and to other relatives or friends.

Should they prepare the whole lesson? No. They may choose any portion of what they have learned. It can be a character, the biblical passages, what they understood from the parable, they can explain the drawing they have colored, or they can use the phrase of the week.

Give them this verse in writing:

But seek first his kingdom and his righteousness, and all these things will be given to you as well.
(Matthew 6:33)

By the way, don't forget to tell them to copy the phrase of the week under the drawing they glued in their journals:

Jesus is worth more than any treasure.

LESSON 5

WORDS ARE SEEDS

God is the author of the Bible, and only the truth it contains will lead people to true happiness.

George Muller

Pinocchio is one of the most famous stories told to children. Many parents, taking advantage of this story, often threaten their children by telling them that their noses will grow if they tell lies. However, what the fairy wanted to tell Pinocchio was more than a threat. She was teaching him a life principle: what we say has consequences and telling the truth is better than telling a lie.

The Bible says that we reap what we sow (Galatians 6:7). And it also uses this image to tell us how important it is to take care of the words that come out of our mouths. If every word we say is like a seed, then what we say to others is like planting it in their hearts.

That's what today's lesson is about.

Let's go!

🧠 AVALANCHE OF IDEAS

ACTIVITY: TONGUE TWISTER

Let's start this class with some tongue twisters that have to do with what we're working on. (Here we propose some but of course if you know others or can come up with something new, go ahead.) As always, pay attention to the age of your children.

You can do this exercise with one or two tongue twisters, or if you prefer with three. Write the sentences on a whiteboard, on a poster, or on a monitor so that the children can read them easily.

Here are some tongue twister options:

- She sells seashells by the seashore.

- This butter's bitter. If I put it in my batter, it will make my batter bitter. But a bit of better butter will make my batter better.

- Sinful Caesar sipped his snifter, seized his knees and sneezed.

Make it like a real contest! Introduce the participants and play fanfare sounds, drums, and applause before and after each person's turn. To make it more exciting, put each participant's name on a piece of paper and then randomly pick each person's turn.

Prepare some prizes for the boys and girls who do best. (And don't forget to have additional prizes in case there are many good entries.) When you announce the winner, give the prize they receive a special name, like "Fastest Tongue in the West Award" or something like that.

If you have many participants, ask them to applaud the winner. And you can ask the winner to say a few words of thanks for this prize.

 FOUNDATIONS OF THE THEME

The most powerful way girls and boys learn is by example. This becomes evident when what they hear anywhere is repeated carelessly in front of other people, without considering the consequences. As they get older, they should learn to choose their words better and to distinguish which things should not be said and the right time to use certain words.

A good disciple must know from a very young age that the words we say are sown in people's hearts and that for this reason we must be careful with our words.

Some common uses of words among many children that we must teach them to avoid are:

- **Lies.** Telling the truth is one of the hallmarks of a good disciple. Although children can often be tempted to lie, part of building the character of Christ in them is helping them always tell the truth regardless of the consequences.

- **Insults.** Most likely, a child who insults another does so because at home they have heard or received insults. This is because the reaction to an insult is most of the time to keep quiet in the moment, but then repeat it against others as a self-defense measure.

- **Teasing.** They are not the same as insults, although they often go together. A person can make fun of another without meaning to insult them, using belittling words or words of disapproval.

- **Gossip.** Talking about someone behind their back is not good. And it does not matter if what is said about the person is true or not, it is still not good to generate or spread gossip. If you're not willing to say in front of the person what you're saying behind their back, then it's best not to say it.

Listening to these things sows nothing good in anyone's heart and it is for this reason that those boys and girls who have received words of disapproval from a very young age believe them and act as if this were true. If they have been told that they are incapable, clumsy, or useless in such and such an area, then they will act in that way because those words have been planted in their hearts.

Warning!

One way to identify that something is happening in children's lives is through their words. If there are problems at home, if someone is harassing them, if they are being bullied, or if they are hanging out with someone who is harmful to them, the best way to notice is to hear the changes in their language. What is being sown in them will inevitably bear fruit!

In the same way, if there is a healthy atmosphere at home, if their friendships are adequate, or if they are receiving Bible teaching well, the fruit of that will be reflected in their words.

Their way of behaving and their reactions will also be a direct consequence of the words they receive. When a child's life is filled with positive words, the results are growth, peace, and love. But when it is filled with negative words, reactions of anger, frustration, and in some cases even violence will occur.

For all this, it is extremely important to teach children to receive the appropriate words and to reject those that are not good for their growth as disciples of Jesus. In turn, as we said before, we must teach them to choose well what words they will sow in the lives of other people.

Now, let's go to the Bible.

📖 FOCUS ON TRUTH

The Word of God is eternal.

In the beginning was the Word, and the Word was with God, and the Word was God.
(John 1:1)

Jesus is the Word of God, the creative essence of God who became man and came to dwell among us.

The Word became flesh and made his dwelling among us. We have seen his glory, the glory of the one and only Son, who came from the Father, full of grace and truth.
(John 1:14)

It is interesting that our planet is called Earth, and that Jesus was sent to live among us here on Earth. If Jesus was the Word of God, and we say that words are seeds, then Jesus was the first seed and the Father decided that he should be planted on Earth.

Jesus used this illustration one day when he said the following:

Very truly I tell you, unless a kernel of wheat falls to the ground and dies, it remains only a single seed. But if it dies, it produces many seeds.
(John 12:24)

Jesus said this to refer to his death. He was the grain of wheat, a seed, that fell to the ground and now had to die. Why? To produce the greatest fruit in all of history: to bring many children of God to the feet of the eternal Father!

Just as we see Jesus illustrated as a lion or a rock on which we can stand firm, so we can also see Jesus as a seed, for he is the Word that is sown in our hearts. We can also see this image of our heart as the earth in which a seed is sown in the parable of the sower:

As he was scattering the seed, some fell along the path, and the birds came and ate it up. Some fell on rocky places, where it did not have much soil. It sprang up quickly, because the soil was shallow. But when the sun

*came up, the plants were scorched, and they withered because they had
no root. Other seed fell among thorns, which grew up and choked the
plants. Still other seed fell on good soil, where it produced a crop—a hundred, sixty or thirty times what was sown.*
(Matthew 13:4-8)

You can read the entire parable to the children, which is found in the book of
Matthew chapter 13. But if possible, it is better to narrate it in your own words to
make it more understandable to the children. If you just read it, you will probably
lose their attention in a few seconds.

LET'S MAKE IT FUN!

Bring a farmer's hat to the meeting. It can be one of those straw ones, or anything that is like what a farmer would use. If you want to make it more attractive,
put on a costume and decorate the room with figures and illustrations from the
countryside.

Also get four types of soil in different containers, and some seeds so that you can
better illustrate what you are going to teach.

The four containers should represent:

1. The land along the path

2. The rocky land

3. The land with thorns

4. The good soil

Now you, dressed like a farmer, will be the one to tell them the story in the first
person:

Hi kids! I am a farmer, and I have come to explain why words are seeds.

Every farmer knows that planting is not easy. The result depends a lot on the soil where the seeds fall.

(Show the children the seeds you brought.)

FAITH STOPS BEING AN INHERITANCE FROM PARENTS AND STARTS BECOMING A PERSONAL COMMITMENT.

The seeds are the Word of God, and each type of soil represents a type of heart.

Below you can read Matthew 13:19-23 so that you can best explain this comparison to the children:

When anyone hears the message about the kingdom and does not understand it, the evil one comes and snatches away what was sown in their heart. This is the seed sown along the path. The seed falling on rocky ground refers to someone who hears the word and at once receives it with joy. But since they have no root, they last only a short time. When trouble or persecution comes because of the word, they quickly fall away. The seed falling among the thorns refers to someone who hears the word, but the worries of this life and the deceitfulness of wealth choke the word, making it unfruitful. But the seed falling on good soil refers to someone who hears the word and understands it. This is the one who produces a crop, yielding a hundred, sixty or thirty times what was sown.
(Matthew 13:19-23)

You can explain it to children like this:

- **The land along the path.** It is a hard land, which represents the hearts of the people who hear the good news of the kingdom of heaven and do not understand it or put it into practice, and that is why they allow themselves to be robbed of the seed they have received.

- **The rocky land.** This is a type of terrain full of rocks. Nothing can grow there because the plants cannot put down deep roots. This ground symbolizes the heart of the people who hear the message and receive it, but do not achieve depth in their experience with God. Therefore, when problems appear their enthusiasm disappears and they turn away from God.

- **The land with thorns.** This is a rough and painful land. It is like the hearts of people who allow themselves to be overwhelmed by everyday things, by money and possessions. Those things do not allow the seed of the Word to grow, and so they move away from God.

- **The good soil.** This is the best type of land. There, the seed can take root and grow. The good soil represents the hearts of the people who receive the gospel of the kingdom of heaven, put it into practice, and go out to announce the message to others.

FROM CHILDHOOD WE MUST BE CAREFUL OF THE WORDS WE SAY BECAUSE WORDS ARE SEEDS.

Ask the children what kind of heart they want to have as you show them again the four containers of dirt that you brought. What we are looking for is that they yearn to have a heart like the good soil, which is fertile and suitable for sowing the Word of God and for it to grow and bear fruit!

After finishing this part, explain to the children that not only is the Word of the kingdom of heaven sown in the heart, but any word can be sown in people! If you lie to someone, that lie is planted in their heart and damages their land. The same happens if you insult someone, or if you make fun of or belittle them.

From childhood we must be careful of the words we say because words are seeds.

To complement this topic you can also use one of these verses:

From the fruit of their mouth a person's stomach is filled; with the harvest of their lips they are satisfied. The tongue has the power of life and death, and those who love it will eat its fruit.
(Proverbs 18:20-21)

Out of the same mouth come praise and cursing. My brothers and sisters, this should not be. Can both fresh water and salt water flow from the same spring?.
(James 3:10-11)

May these words of my mouth and this meditation of my heart be pleasing in your sight, lord, my Rock and my Redeemer.
(Psalms 19:14)

INTROSPECTION

Help the boys and girls to understand well the key phrase of this lesson and the reason why they should keep this in mind.

I take care of my words because they are seeds.

Their understanding of the topic will depend a lot on how much they have understood from the previous section, but you can also ask them questions so they can respond at an age-appropriate level:

- What kind of heart would you like to have to receive God's Word?

- Why should you take care of your words spoken to other people?

- How could you sow something bad in someone?

- How could you sow something good in someone?

- How do you take care of your heart from the words you hear that don't build you up?

 REFLECT ON A CHARACTER

PINOCCHIO

Pinocchio was a wooden puppet who wanted with all his might to be a real boy. His problem? He was very deceitful. Every time he got in trouble he would tell a lie so as not to be found out, and when he did that, his nose would grow longer and longer.

Pinocchio went through many adventures, including something similar to what happened to Jonah: Pinocchio was swallowed by a whale!

At the end of the story, a fairy grants Pinocchio his wish to become a real boy and be happy with his creator, Geppetto.

Pinocchio had to learn his lessons the hard way... and of course we are talking about an old tale, but this story is still used today so that children can reflect.

How crazy it would be if our words produced effects in our body. Right? Imagine, for example, that every time you insult or make fun of someone, your hair turns blue. Or that your eyes grow when you tell a lie. Or that when you speak ill of someone behind their back, your skin turns green.

In this world that will not happen, but we will have the voice of the Holy Spirit to guide us. He can help us control the words that are going to come out of our mouths, as well as warn us when we have used inappropriate words, and even guide us to ask for forgiveness.

The Holy Spirit can also help us recognize when we have received words from other people that may hurt us, so that we can uproot those bad seeds before they take root in our hearts.

QUESTIONS FOR YOUR DISCIPLES:

- What can you do so that bad seeds do not come out of your mouth toward other people?

- What can you do when you hear words that hurt you?

MIRIAM, MOSES'S SISTER

There was an occasion when Miriam, the sister of Moses, along with her brother Aaron, began to gossip about their brother and leader. They did not agree with the wife that Moses had chosen, and because of that they spoke ill of him behind his back.

It was already known that the Hebrew people continually complained because they did not have all the comforts they would have wanted while walking through the desert. They complained because they were thirsty, and Moses drew water from a rock. They complained that they had no food, and God sent them manna from heaven. They later complained because manna was the only thing they ate, and God sent them quail. It was not once but several times that God's people complained, and when they did, many gossiped about Moses's abilities as a leader. And although at every opportunity God demonstrated to them that he was with Moses and endorsed his leadership, still they did not stop gossiping.

God had to teach them a lesson through Miriam. When she began to gossip against Moses, leprosy suddenly appeared on her skin, and because of that she had to be separated from everyone for seven days.

It's not the same as Pinocchio, but this story shows us that God is listening to us all the time. And although a disease will not come to us or be noticed on our skin, we must be aware that our words can have consequences.

QUESTIONS FOR YOUR DISCIPLES:

- How would you feel if you found out that a friend or sibling of yours criticized you behind your back?

- Have you ever criticized someone behind their back? What can you do to remedy this, or to prevent it from happening again?

 # MOBILIZE

Ask your children's parents to choose a system of rewards for well-planted words, or design a system that you can reward them in the next class.

The idea is that for a week the children should look every day for a person in whom to sow good words. Of course, as a discipler you must be sure that the children have understood the concept of sowing words of blessing, or positive words, before doing this exercise.

Explain that in their DISCIPLE'S JOURNAL they should make a chart to record the name of the person to whom they said something positive, the words they said, and the day they said it. Every time they have met their goal for the day, they must make a mark in their box, and then they will receive their reward.

The rewards for each goal achieved can be a piece of candy, a coin, a sticker, or some other small prize.

This is the table that you can photocopy or that they can copy in their journals:

DAY	PERSON	WORDS	Check if the daily goal is completed
MONDAY	Example: My brother	I told him he is a good student.	

TUESDAY			
WEDNESDAY			
THURSDAY			
FRIDAY			

If parents are participating, you can suggest that they keep this reward system going longer. That will depend on each family. As for you as a discipler, your goal will be for them to be able to do it all week until the next meeting.

Also remind them to copy the phrase of the week:

I take care of my words because they are seeds.

Do not forget to encourage them to decorate the pages of the journal to their liking. They can draw pictures of people receiving their kind words, and how they felt. Or they can record how it felt to say good words about others.

Before ending the meeting, pray for the boys and girls in your group, so that they can remember that the words that come out of their mouths are seeds, and learn to take care of them.

This has been a very important lesson. Let's keep moving forward together!

FACE YOUR FEARS

Fear is a reaction. Bravery is a choice.
Winston Churchill

We all experience anxieties and fears. Fear is real regardless of its reasons and even when its reasons are only in our mind. We start with this statement because one of the worst fears of many Christians is expressing that they feel anxiety or fear. In essence, we are afraid of fear, which happens to us not only with this emotion, but even with sadness, and proof of that is how quickly we tell someone who has lost a family member that "God uses all things for good" so that they no longer feel sad. Fear is natural and even positive because it emerges from our instinct for self-preservation and love for life. It is even an expression of the love we have for others. When it becomes negative is when it takes control of us and governs our emotions, or worse, it makes our decisions. It happens with any temptation. It is one thing for an attractive person to catch your eye and another to stop to look at that person with lust. As is often said in this case, the problem is in the second glance, and children must learn that fear is natural and how to overcome it by putting our trust in the Lord.

Prepare the boys and girls beforehand, warning them that in today's lesson we will talk about courage. Today, we will learn to face our fears!

🧠 AVALANCHE OF IDEAS

ACTIVITY: IDENTIFY FEAR

Arrange the boys and girls in a line, one next to the other, all facing you. Explain to them that you are going to mention some fears, and that you need them to be very honest when answering. When you mention each of the fears on the following list, those who think they have that fear should take a step forward.

ONE OF THE BEST REMEDIES TO GET RID OF FEAR IS TO TELL OTHERS ABOUT IT.

Tell them that this is an experiment to measure the fear levels of the group. (By talking as a group, you will lower any concern they might feel about being evaluated individually.) Get a magnifying glass or a lab coat to look like a scientist, and that will make it feel more real.

Remind them of the importance of telling the truth, as we saw in the previous lesson. Usually, fear is something that people want to hide, but one of the best remedies to get rid of fear is to tell others about it.

Start reading the list, pausing after each sentence to give them time to think.

I am afraid...

- Of public speaking.

- Of heights.

- Of being alone.

- Of water or swimming.

- Of dogs that bark loudly.

- Of something happening to the people that I love.

- Of the dark.

- Of not having friends.

- Of other people's criticism.

As you bring up each of the points, ask the children to step forward if that is something that scares them even a little. You can take notes in a notebook of how many children identify with each fear but make it clear to them that you are only writing down the total number and not their names, so they do not feel intimidated.

The number is not that important, but you should watch their body language, even those who did not step forward. As a good discipler, you must learn to look at the attitudes of your boys and girls to discern if they are telling the truth or not. In many cases, they will feel tempted not to take the step forward precisely for fear of what others will say.

This exercise will teach them to be more honest with themselves and with others, and, above all, you will be able to get to know them and help them better when dealing with these types of topics that are not so common for a class.

End by sharing the results of the "investigation" with the group. They won't be personal results, like we already said, so you'll say something like: "Our discipleship class must learn to face various fears, mainly the fear of swimming, the dark, and being alone."

Let's work on facing our fears.

 FOUNDATIONS OF THE THEME

Fear is an intense emotion that allows us to react to some danger or threat. A barking dog can cause a certain level of fear, enough to cross to the other side of the street but if we were to meet a tiger, we would surely feel much more afraid. Probably so afraid that we would run at the maximum possible speed! This happens with situations of real danger, but it can also happen with imaginary situations and therein lies one of the foundational aspects: to control fear so that it does not control us.

So, if fear itself is not bad, since it helps us protect ourselves and ward off danger, what is the problem? The problem is that when it grows too much, or when it arises due to unreal things, it is a barrier that prevents us from moving forward. That is the fear we must overcome.

Why talk about fear with children?

FEAR ITSELF IS NOT BAD. THE PROBLEM IS THAT WHEN IT GROWS TOO MUCH, OR WHEN IT ARISES DUE TO UNREAL THINGS, IT IS A BARRIER THAT PREVENTS US FROM MOVING FORWARD.

Because fear is limiting. It stops dreams and incapacitates children, reducing the chances of them being effective in the kingdom of heaven. Children often do not grow in different areas, such as service or worship, because they are afraid of not being able to, of not being accepted, of what others say, etc.

Healthy children believe that they can improve the lives of others and do not have the fears that we have as adults. As parents we must be wise and not stifle those desires and dreams of our children. This is the age when you feel that everything you imagine can become reality.
Elisa Shannon Brown *(Trabajemos en familia) [Let's work as a family]*

That is precisely why we must talk about fear. So that our children do not inherit our own limitations.

In order to overcome it, we must first understand that fear moves in cycles. It originates with a bad experience that we do not want to repeat. The fear of repeating that experience later produces an inability to react appropriately. That inability causes us to have a bad experience again, and thus the cycle repeats itself.

This is what the cycle of fear looks like:

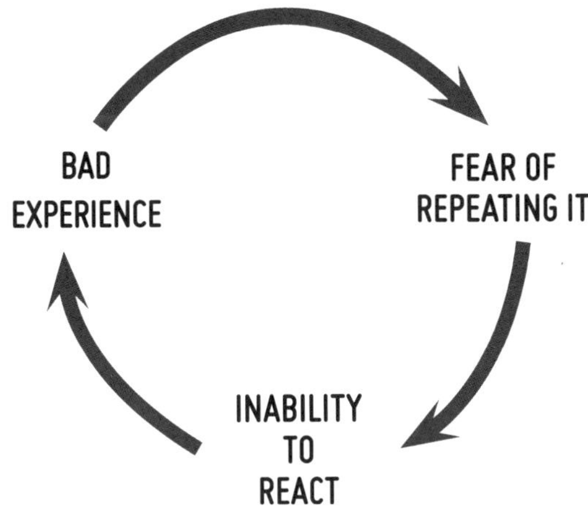

For example:

- A person throws a child into the pool to learn to swim.

- The child cannot swim, and almost drowns.

- The child does not want to repeat that experience again, and that is why they are afraid of the water.

- Even when they are older, they cannot learn to swim, or at least it is very difficult for them.

- Every time they enter a pool, that fear will return.

Understanding this cycle of fear makes us see how important it is to discuss the issue with our children. Many of the attitudes that adults have are caused by some type of fear that they feel and that they have not been able to resolve, and this shapes their behavior, preventing them from being free. The fear then becomes a prison that keeps the person incarcerated for their entire life and does not allow them to be what they have been called to be.

Steps to facing fears:

IDENTIFY THE FEAR.

- Explore the moment when it appeared in your life.

- Remember how you reacted in that moment.

- Understand the parts of that fear that only exist in your mind.

- Go to the Word of God to put the real foundation of your confidence and security in the Lord.

- Take concrete steps to free yourself from fear.

Here is a practical example that you can use to explain the topic to children:

Once you have identified what fear you want to face, you must remember when and under what circumstances it appeared in your life. Observe the feelings that scene still causes in you when you remember it. When seeking to understand which factors are only in your mind, try to have an objective judgment. In the swimming example, the factor only in the mind would be thinking that you could drown in a pool where you can stand on the bottom and have your head above the water with no problem. In this way you can clearly verify that your fear is not real. Then you must go to God and ask for strength, courage, and protection to face that fear and be free from it. You will take small steps at first, until little by little you will free yourself!

Of course, each case will be different, but this is at least a general idea of how to face the fears that we recognize in our lives.

We will be much freer and happier without them!

What about aggressive dogs, or being near the edge of a tall building's terrace? Well, there are fears that are logical and help protect us from danger. But there are others that are not good because they limit us. Being afraid of water prevents us from learning to swim, and that takes away from a good experience that we could enjoy! That is why it is good to learn from a young age to differentiate the fears that serve to take care of ourselves from those that hold us back and prevent us from growing.

📖 FOCUS ON TRUTH

Several times Jesus told his disciples not to be afraid. One of the most famous passages is when Jesus walked on the water. The disciples were in a boat in the middle of rough waters, and suddenly someone appeared walking on the water. Of course, the first thing they thought was that it was a ghost! Jesus had to yell at them to not be afraid, it was him!

Immediately Jesus made the disciples get into the boat and go on ahead of him to the other side, while he dismissed the crowd. After he had dismissed them, he went up on a mountainside by himself to pray. Later that night, he was there alone, and the boat was already a considerable distance from land, buffeted by the waves because the wind was against it.

Shortly before dawn Jesus went out to them, walking on the lake. When the disciples saw him walking on the lake, they were terrified. "It's a ghost," they said, and cried out in fear.

But Jesus immediately said to them: "Take courage! It is I. Don't be afraid."

"Lord, if it's you," Peter replied, "tell me to come to you on the water."

"Come," he said.

Then Peter got down out of the boat, walked on the water and came toward Jesus.

(Matthew 14:22-29)

Sometimes when we see supernatural things, we may think that the forces of the enemy are stronger because of the fear they produce. But in this passage, we can learn several things:

- **Jesus is supernatural.** That means that he is above natural things and can do anything.

- **Jesus can overcome any fear.** There is nothing so great that Jesus cannot overcome it!

- **Jesus tells us that we can also overcome any fear.** If we are united with Jesus, we can face fear with his help.

IT IS NOT ABOUT PRETENDING THAT FEAR DOES NOT EXIST, BUT ABOUT BEING ABLE TO MOVE ON FROM IT.

Walking on water in this case represents walking on fear. It is not about pretending that fear does not exist, but about being able to move on from it. This means that although fear exists, it should not control us, but we must control fear and submit it to Christ.

Usually, when fear invades us, it is because we are deceived in the mind to think things contrary to what God has told us.

Look at this other passage:

For the Spirit God gave us does not make us timid, but gives us power, love and self-discipline.
(2 Timothy 1:7)

It is important that your boys and girls know that God has given them a spirit that can overcome fear, because it is a spirit full of supernatural and divine strength, love, and self-control.

 INTROSPECTION

The key phrase of this lesson will serve to affirm in the boys and girls what they have learned:

With Jesus I can overcome fear.

Remember that your job is to help them think, and then to believe. We don't want them to believe blindly, because that kind of faith runs out quickly.

QUESTIONS TO REFLECT ON:

- What does it mean to walk with Jesus?
- When fear comes, how can I overcome it with his help?

REFLECT ON A CHARACTER

Remember that this section can be used as you wish. You may choose to use both characters, or just one of them to illustrate the theme. It may also be that you do not want to use any, or that you prefer to choose another example that seems more appropriate for your group. The choice is yours!

On the other hand, keep in mind that when it comes to movie characters, it is a good alternative to have a video ready with the trailer or some scenes from it. This is helpful to activate the senses and keep children interested and attentive.

THE CROODS

The story of this film takes place in a prehistoric time, when human beings were just learning to defend themselves against the things of the world. They had to deal with natural disasters, earthquakes, huge animals, and many other things.

The Croods are a family from that time, and they have gotten used to living inside a cave. No one can stray too far, and the general rule is to be afraid of everything. Grug, the patriarch, the father of the family, has taught them this.

Then Guy appears, a boy who comes from outside, and who has investigated the world and has learned to overcome all the obstacles that have come his way. Guy no longer lives in fear like the Croods. He lives in freedom!

QUESTIONS FOR YOUR DISCIPLES:

- What fears do you have?

- What fears do your family members have?

- Are there any fears that you have "learned" from your family?

- Do you think you can be free from those fears? How?

PETER

The Bible hides nothing, and it has not been a problem for any of the biblical writers to describe in detail what really happened. This is another of the arguments that make the Word of God reliable and true.

It is said that Peter was very close to Jesus. From the day his spiritual eyes were opened and he became certain that Jesus was the Christ, everything in Peter's life changed. Peter had been an impetuous and strong fisherman, capable of shouldering all the hard work that his trade required. Because of that same strong character, Peter was the one who asked the questions that the others did not dare to ask, and he had more initiative than the rest of his friends. All of that was positive, but he also had to deal with aspects of his character that he couldn't seem to control. Peter was impulsive, to the point that in a fit of anger he decided to cut off the ear of one of those who wanted to arrest his Master! Jesus had to correct his abrupt reaction by performing a miracle and reattaching the man's ear.

It was also Peter who denied Jesus, although shortly before he had confidently said that he would never leave him alone.

Peter was impetuous and strong-willed. However, the Bible tells us of an occasion in which Peter had to face fear. It was night, and the disciples were in a boat fighting against the wind and rough waters. Suddenly, Jesus appeared to them walking on the water. They thought it was a ghost, but Jesus told them not to be afraid, and that it was him. Peter then told him that if it really was the Master, he would order him to walk to where he was. Jesus did so, and Peter began to walk on the water...until he realized what he was doing and saw how huge the waves were all around him. What happened then? Peter felt afraid and began to sink. "Lord, save me!" he cried out to Jesus. And the Bible tells us that, reaching out his hand, Jesus caught him. Of course, everyone in the boat was amazed and recognized that Jesus truly was the Son of God!

From this story we can learn that when we are afraid, if we cry out to Jesus, he will take us by the hand and help us.

QUESTIONS FOR YOUR DISCIPLES:

- What was it that made Peter almost sink?

- What did Peter do to save himself?

- What did Jesus do when Peter asked him for help?

- What can you do when you are afraid, and what do you think Jesus will do?

MOBILIZE

How do we overcome fear? Use the weapons that the Bible gives us to defeat it!

To close this lesson, teach your children these four powerful biblical concepts:

1. Truth defeats fear.

To the Jews who had believed him, Jesus said, "If you hold to my teaching, you are really my disciples. Then you will know the truth, and the truth will set you free."
(John 8:31-32)

Knowing the truth, which is Jesus, allows us to be free from many things, including fear. If we do not know the truth of God expressed through Christ, we will remain in fear.

2. Love defeats fear.

There is no fear in love. But perfect love drives out fear, because fear has to do with punishment. The one who fears is not made perfect in love.
(1 John 4:18)

If the perfect love that comes from God is real, then we know that fear will be cast out, because God is love. If God is in us, there is no room for fear.

3. Faith defeats fear.

And without faith it is impossible to please God, because anyone who comes to him must believe that he exists and that he rewards those who earnestly seek him.
(Hebrews 11:6)

Without faith it is impossible to please God; therefore, fear can be a manifestation of lack of faith, or disbelief. Developing our faith and putting it into practice makes us overcome all fear!

4. Courage defeats fear.

Have I not commanded you? Be strong and courageous. Do not be afraid; do not be discouraged, for the lord your God will be with you wherever you go.
(Joshua 1:9)

God has already ordered it: we must not be afraid or let circumstances discourage us. The Lord commands us to be strong and courageous!

Now let's go to the DISCIPLE'S JOURNAL!

During the week the children must take a photograph or draw a picture that represents one of these four weapons that we have against fear. (Or if you want, you can draw all four!)

To choose the picture or drawing, the following questions could be asked:

- How does truth defeat fear?

- How does love defeat fear?

- How can faith defeat fear?

- How does courage defeat fear?

Don't forget to bring parents up to speed on this assignment so they too can put these principles into practice at home.

Before finishing, remember to ask the children to write down the phrase of the week in their journals:

With Jesus I can overcome fear.

Pray that your boys and girls can hold hands with Jesus and move through life free from fear!

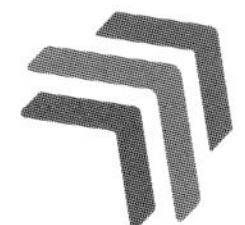

LESSON 7

THE CRISIS OF SHAME

Shame is a dark lens that doesn't let you see the brightness of the light.

Valeria Leys

Shame originates from the feeling of vulnerability, and it is interesting that the Bible mentions it from the outset as Adam and Eve's reaction to their sin. However, it does not always have to do with sin but with some experience that later prevents us from clearly saying our "no" and "yes" and expressing our opinions and feelings. For this reason, as we learned with fear, we must learn to manage shame and keep it under control.

Shame can be caused by numerous factors. It can be a consequence of a lack of conformity, guilt, secrets, status, or competition and it can prevent us from growing, doing what is right, or what is best for our development. That is why shame is another important issue for children.

 AVALANCHE OF IDEAS

ACTIVITY: COMPETING EMOTIONS

Plan a contest to see who is best at interpreting human emotions. For this, you must prepare posters or pictures that express the different emotions that we can experience.

- If we are happy, we laugh like crazy. (laughing image)

- If we get hit, we complain. (complaint image)

- If something saddens us, we cry. (crying image)

- If we are ashamed, we blush and want to hide. (image of shame)

Explain to the group that today they are going to explore some of the emotions that human beings feel. Next, show them one by one the images you prepared, and tell them that as the images are shown, they should imitate them, but it should always be in an exaggerated way. Show the pictures faster and faster. This will mix up the interpretations of the different emotions and is sure to get some laughs.

After this warm-up, tell them a story like the following, and tell them that when they hear a reaction, they should interpret it the same way: very exaggerated. Warn them that there will be prizes at the end for the best performers!

Here is the story:

I was walking down the street and I saw a clown who made everyone **LAUGH** *with his juggling. People* **LAUGHED** *and* **LAUGHED**. *A man who was walking by, staring at the clown, did not look where he was going and hit his head against a wall. "Oh, oh!", the injured gentleman* **COMPLAINED** *of pain. While he* **COMPLAINED** *of pain holding his head in his hands, everyone made fun of him. They* **LAUGHED** *like crazy, no longer at the clown, but now at the poor man who hit his head.*

The man **STARTED BLUSHING** *from* **SHAME,** *and he tried to* **HIDE HIS FACE** *so that no one would see him. But everyone kept making fun of him, so he began to* **CRY.** *He* **CRIED AND CRIED**.

A good old woman who was also there approached the man, extended her hand with a **SMILE,** *and said: "Worse things have happened to me!" It brought joy back to the man, who then simply* **LAUGHED** *at what had happened to him.*

If you want to give the activity a bigger challenge, take the different images and place them on the ground. The challenge will be that when you tell the story, the children must imitate the emotion, but also run to step on the sheet with the correct image. You will see that some will do it faster than others, and that many in a hurry will get confused and run to the wrong card. Don't stop the story; keep telling it and put a strong emphasis on each word that refers to an emotion.

If your meeting is virtual, you can show the images to the camera and ask the children to leave the microphone open so you can listen to each other's performances. You will have to take a few breaks until the children stop laughing or crying, but it will be a lot of fun. The effect will also be similar, and the delivery of prizes can be through images on the screen.

Here's a suggested list of prizes to hand out:

- Prize for the best laugh.

- Prize for the most painful pain complaint.

- Prize for crying with the greatest sadness.

- Prize for the best performance of blushing and hiding from shame.

📝 FOUNDATIONS OF THE THEME

Shame is one of those emotions that can haunt us from childhood to adulthood. No one is safe from going through moments of shame, because life will always put us in situations that could embarrass us. That is exactly why we need to learn to deal with those emotions, face them, and overcome them!

It is a challenge for every discipler to be able to gain the confidence of the boys and girls to be able to discuss openly topics about feelings and emotions. Especially in the case of shame, which usually causes discomfort and a tendency to want to hide what you feel.

Let's learn what happens with children:

- They have little ability to deal with emotional issues. At this stage they are just learning to assimilate negative feelings, and they are still confused about how other people's actions, reactions and emotions work. And how their own work.

- They learn to put up barriers. When a boy or girl goes through an embarrassing situation, they tend to hide it. They do not want to talk about it, and it is very difficult for them to relate this situation with the values they have learned.

- They focus on their shortcomings. A situation of shame makes the child fix their gaze on themself and point to a certain part of their being as the culprit or the person responsible for that situation.

- They have diverse emotional reactions. Every child is different. Some can isolate themselves, others become victims of any circumstance, and others can live in fear, or become tyrants and exercise power or violence.

Warning!

Once we open a topic like this, it is likely that we will encounter serious situations such as sexual abuse, domestic violence, and other issues that will be difficult to face. In such cases, we suggest contacting experienced psychological or biblical counselors to address these issues further.

WHY IS IT IMPORTANT TO ADDRESS THE ISSUE OF SHAME?

As it happens a lot in children, and even teens, people keep many of the things that happen in their inner being to themselves. This can affect them in their future, in the development of their personality, and even in the way they will face the problems and crises that they will experience years later. In fact, many adults manifest problems in their relationships, in their behavior, at work, etc., just because they have unfinished issues that they did not successfully overcome in these early stages of life. It is important that you as a discipler know that if you are made aware of child abuse you must report it to the authorities.

In addition, since today the issue of bullying is so present in all sectors of society, it is important to give children tools so that they learn to defend themselves, in a good way, from this type of social attack.

Some situations that can cause shame in children are:

- **Not meeting social expectations.** Not making friends in their social environment can cause them to feel that no one wants or accepts them.

- **Bullying and other forms of harassment.** This is one of the situations that produce the greatest shame among children. The fact of being disturbed by someone who denigrates you on any level is not a light thing.

- **School failure.** Getting a question wrong, getting the lowest grade in class, saying something wrong in front of everyone-any of these situations is very embarrassing.

- **An embarrassing experience.** A fall in front of everyone, tearing or wetting their pants by accident, or anything that exposes them in front of others-all these situations are experienced with great anguish by children.

All children subjected to circumstances like the ones mentioned or similar are experiencing conflicts of anxiety and guilt that it is easier for them to channel into a reaction against the school than to direct it against the older people directly.
(Pedagogía y Psicología Infantil: El período escolar) [Pedagogy and Child Psychology: The school period]

HOW DOES A BOY OR GIRL HANDLE SHAME?

Embarrassing situations are interpreted by children in the form of rejection. Therefore, the most common reaction to them is the same: rejection.

This rejection can manifest itself in different ways:

- They avoid hanging out with other children.

- They begin to hate going to school.

- They refuse to talk about the topic that overwhelms them.

- They can become shy and withdrawn.

EMBARRASSING SITUATIONS ARE INTERPRETED BY CHILDREN IN THE FORM OF REJECTION. THEREFORE, THE MOST COMMON REACTION TO THEM IS THE SAME: REJECTION.

Shame is related to low self-esteem and low self-confidence. Your job as a discipler is to help children build a healthy self-esteem and a positive self-perception.

The subject of self-perception is complex, and it is key in the human being in general, but more in the consolidation of the young people who are being formed. If the self-perception of a child is damaged, hurt, or violated, this will bring consequences in their development, behavior, and interaction with others.
Laura Gutiérrez *(Manual de consejería para niños) [Counseling manual for children]*

This section has given you ideas around which you can have important conversations with the parents of your children, and has given you the information that you will need as a discipler to guide children to a life free from the bondage of shame. Now it's time to teach them!

📖 FOCUS ON TRUTH

What does the Bible say about shame?

The first time shame is mentioned is in this passage from the book of Genesis:

Adam and his wife were both naked, and they felt no shame.
(Genesis 2:25)

Before eating the forbidden fruit, that is, before sinning, we see that Adam and Eve

- Were free of shame.

- Were naked but didn't feel shame. But then, what happened?

At that moment their eyes were opened, and they suddenly felt shame at their nakedness. So they sewed fig leaves together to cover themselves.
(Genesis 3:7 NLT))

After eating the forbidden fruit, that is, when they sinned, Adam and Eve

- Were ashamed.

- Hid from God.

- Had to find leaves to cover themselves.

That's when shame appeared! And yes, it was a consequence of sin! Therefore, every time we disobey God, we have that kind of desire to hide, just like Adam and Eve did.

From there, shame spread throughout the world, and today it is one of the tools the enemy uses the most to stop us. If he manages to make us feel ashamed, then he knows that this will limit us and prevent us from fulfilling God's purpose in our lives!

Now, read with your children the following passage:

You have made us a reproach to our neighbors, the scorn and derision of those around us. You have made us a byword among the nations; the peoples shake their heads at us. I live in disgrace all day long, and my face is covered with shame at the taunts of those who reproach and revile me, because of the enemy, who is bent on revenge.
(Psalm 44:13-16)

The person who wrote this psalm felt very ashamed, because all the other villages made fun of him. Maybe bullying has been around longer than we think!

Have you ever felt overwhelmed by a feeling of shame?

There are many passages in Scripture that speak of shame, but in the end, if we are looking for a solution, it all points directly to Jesus. The Bible says that he was the one who took away our shame. Share this verse with your children:

Fixing our eyes on Jesus, the pioneer and perfecter of faith. For the joy set before him he endured the cross, scorning its shame, and sat down at the right hand of the throne of God.
(Hebrews 12:2)

Jesus is our role model. He perfects our faith when he makes us see that he has already loaded all shame on his shoulders.

The way Jesus died was humiliating and shameful.

Why was Jesus crucified naked? So that he could take away the shame of nakedness that came from the time of Adam and Eve.

Today we are part of that humanity that has been rescued from the punishment of death and the shame of the world, to be welcomed into the kingdom of the Son of God (Colossians 1:13).

Explain this to your children: If Jesus could take all the shame on himself, and rise from the grave in victory, then we can look to him to rid us of all shame and help us overcome those feelings of embarrassment that could haunt us.

That is why we must keep our eyes fixed on him!

TO TALK THROUGH WITH YOUR CHILDREN:

What things could embarrass you?

- Being treated badly or made fun of by someone.

- That you do poorly in school.

- Feeling that others don't accept you, or not feeling part of the group.

- Committing a sin that brings you shame before God.

What should you do in each case?

- If someone treats you badly or makes fun of you, you must learn to forgive them and not hold a grudge against them. Forgiveness will bring you freedom from shame!

- If you got bad grades and because of that you feel inadequate or unintelligent, you should know that the grades do not reflect who you really are. In fact, you are a very valuable person! The grade you get in a subject can be low, but it can also change and improve. That doesn't change who you really are.

- If you feel that you are not accepted in a group, do not resent them. Most people who tend to reject others do so because they have also been rejected. You must prevent this from affecting you and learn not to reject anyone else.

- When you sin, you must repent and ask God for forgiveness. The guilt and shame you feel for having done something wrong will go away when you receive forgiveness from your heavenly Father.

 INTROSPECTION

We are going to do a reflection exercise, but this time it will not be about one but about several sentences, and we will do it in a fun way: with the "true or false" game!

Copy the sentences on a board or read them one by one while you give the boys and girls time to think and respond:

- When there is something that embarrasses me, I must hide it so that no one finds out.

- Shame will haunt me forever.

- The feeling of shame can be defeated thanks to Jesus.

- Shame is not important; I shouldn't listen to it.

- Shame and guilt are the same thing.

You can explain each sentence and then let the children give their reasons why they chose one answer or another. Help them understand if you see that they are confused at any point.

The key phrase for the children to learn this week is:

Jesus took all my shame.

Later they will write it down in their journals so they don't forget it.

REFLECT ON A CHARACTER

HICCUP

Hiccup was a teenager from the Viking village Berk, who had grown up full of complexities. Berk was an island where all the Vikings grew up learning to be the

148

strongest warriors. But Hiccup was different. He didn't have as many muscles as the other boys his age, and for that he suffered the ridicule of the entire town. They all trained to hunt dragons, and seeing Hiccup, no one would have believed that he could defend the town from any dragon that attacked them.

In fact, Hiccup made friends with the dragons, but first, he had to fight against everyone's disapproval. Hiccup didn't fit in with the group. He was different, and simply for that reason he was not well-liked. Everyone rejected him, and the boy ended up in a prison of shame and self-condemnation.

Hiccup was an insecure boy, and like many boys his age nowadays, he didn't feel the freedom to talk about this with his father or anyone else. Even later in the movie, when he was able to tame a one-of-a-kind dragon, Hiccup still didn't feel like he was fit to be considered a true Viking.

Being the laughingstock of the town brought a great shame to Hiccup's heart that made him unable to face life's problems. He suffered because of who he was and how others saw him. Fortunately, throughout the film we can see his process of abandoning shame and insecurity to become what he had been called to be: a great dragon trainer.

QUESTIONS FOR YOUR DISCIPLES:

- Have you ever felt ashamed like Hiccup? In what circumstance, and what caused that feeling?

- Do you think that shame dominates any aspect of your life? Which one(s) and why?

- What do you think you could do to be free from shame?

JOHN THE BAPTIST

Jesus knew John from before he was born, when they were both in their mothers' wombs. Although Scripture does not mention much about his childhood and adolescence, it is very likely that, as the son of Mary's cousin, John was someone very close to Jesus in his childhood years. Already having reached youth or adulthood, John reappears in the Bible as someone who has received God's instruction to begin baptizing all who wish to approach him.

John was walking in the desert and there he was baptizing people. His clothes were made of camel hair, and his food was wild honey and locusts (not the marine crustacean, but huge crickets).

JOHN DID NOT SEEM TO CARE ABOUT HIS IMAGE OR WHAT OTHERS MIGHT THINK OF HIM. JOHN CARED MORE ABOUT HIS PURPOSE.

With only this brief description we can realize that he was a person that the rest would consider "strange." His clothes and his food were not something common in his time, nor was his way of living in the desert like a hermit. His preaching was harsh, but nevertheless John led many to repent and turn to God. Thus, it was necessary for it to happen, since this man came to prepare the way for the arrival of the Messiah.

It is interesting to note that John did not seem to care about his image or what others might think of him. John cared more about his purpose, that for which he had been called by God. Most likely, a lot of people were talking bad about him behind his back, but that didn't stop him at all! John was so committed to his call that he decided to ignore any of the strategies the enemy used to try to stop him.

The example of John the Baptist is powerful. He avoided being overcome by shame because he considered his calling more valuable than what others could say about him. He did not seek the approval of men. More important than what he wore or what he ate was what he had come to do for the kingdom of God.

QUESTIONS FOR YOUR DISCIPLES:

- Have you felt ashamed of the way you dress or what you do? If so, when?

- Have you felt that your image is more important than your purpose? If so, when?

- What example can we take from John the Baptist in this regard?

 # MOBILIZE

Tell your children to take their DISCIPLE'S JOURNAL and write down the phrase of the week:

Jesus took all my shame.

Then ask them to draw the following diagram, which we will call "the circle of trust". The idea is that they can place themselves in the center of a circle in which they are surrounded by people they can trust.

Here is the basic format of the chart, but ideally, they should fill in each circle with the names of specific people. They can do it alone or with help from their parents at home if families are joining you in this discipleship effort.

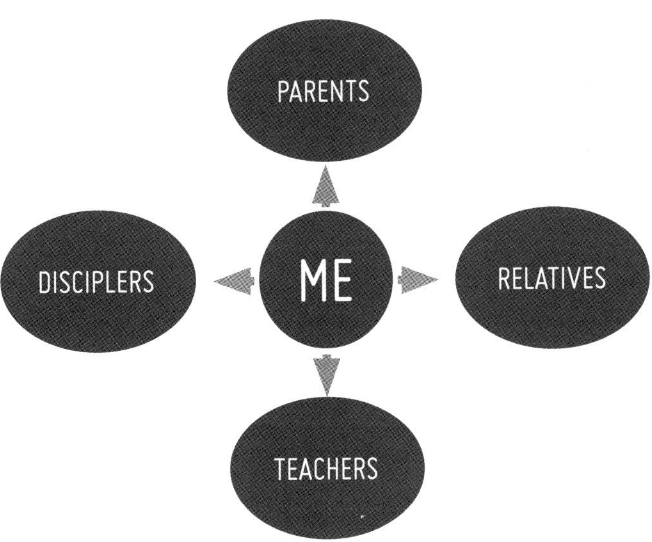

Finally, here is a list of tips that would be good to share with your children:

IF THERE IS SOMEONE WHO IS EMBARRASSING THEM

- Train your children so they know who they can count on in their family. Tell them to go back to the circle of trust to share with someone what is happening.

- Let them know that they can count on you too. That's why it's important that you're in the circle!

- Teach them to handle different situations.

- Tell them that feelings are not good or bad; they are natural reactions of the human being to the things that happen to us.

- Explain to them that it's normal to feel embarrassed about something, but if someone is bothering them, they need to tell someone so they can stop it.

- Teach them that it is important to know how to say no. No one can touch them improperly or ask them to do things that are not right.

- Encourage them to make a commitment to tell their parents or leaders about anything embarrassing so they can help them.

IF THEY FEEL EMBARRASSED BY SOMETHING WRONG THEY DID

- Let them know that God is always ready to forgive us. If they tell you how they feel about doing something wrong, are sorry, and ask for forgiveness, they can be sure that God will forgive them.

- Teach them to pray so that they learn to ask Jesus to take away their shame for having sinned.

- Tell them that it is not necessary to live forever with guilt. We cannot continue to feel guilty for something we did, if we have already asked God for forgiveness. You have to receive that forgiveness and know that God is faithful to his promise.

LAST TIPS FOR THE DISCIPLER

- Communicate with empathy. Do not let children feel that you are scared by what they tell you, or that you will turn on the alarm to expose them. Make them feel confident.

- Respect their space. Never force a child to tell you something they don't want to. Rather, gain enough confidence that at some point they will open up to you.

- Analyze the seriousness of the cases. A case of bullying is not the same as a case of sexual abuse. Sometimes you will have to ask for help or report the situation to parents or law enforcement.

- Count on a team of professionals such as psychologists, counselors, or therapists whom you can recommend to the family in the most serious cases.

- Accompany your children in their conflict. You won't be able to solve all their problems but you will be able to accompany them while they are being solved.

End the lesson by praying that each of your boys and girls will have a real encounter with Jesus that will allow them to live free from the shackles of shame.

THE VALUE OF FRIENDSHIP

Friendship is born at that moment when one person says to another: "You too? I thought I was the only one."

C. S. Lewis

If you have read that story, you will know that the knight in rusty armor suffered much hardship when his armor stuck to his body. He thought he had a perfect life, but this fact made him realize that he was alone, not because the others had distanced themselves, but because he had pushed everyone away. He thought he was a good father and husband, but he was very wrong. It wasn't until he made some friends while searching for a solution to his problem that he was able to understand what was wrong with his life.

Friends are important in the development of a person. That is why one of the great goals that we have as disciplers is to help our boys and girls to choose their friends well.

The knight in this story, unable to remove his rusty armor, had to rely on his new friends for eating, drinking, raising his spirits, and giving him advice. It's not about having a lot of friends, it's about having the right friends!

IT'S NOT ABOUT HAVING A LOT OF FRIENDS, IT'S ABOUT HAVING THE RIGHT FRIENDS!

Therefore, today we will talk about friendship and the value it has.

🧠 AVALANCHE OF IDEAS

This part of the lesson is intended to help children activate their senses and focus on the topic that will be discussed. It must be a dynamic and different activity, creative enough to give them the desire to learn, but always pointing to the topic that will be discussed.

ACTIVITY: MY PLAYMATE

For this activity you should ask the children in advance to each bring to the meeting a doll that they have at home and that they consider special. Any toy that they can interact with while playing will be fine.

You must also bring a doll or puppet and lead the meeting with it; the doll you bring will become the teacher. Speak as if you were the doll, in a voice that is fun for children. If you don't feel up to it, invite a teen or young adult who can do it for you.

To start the meeting, everyone should present their doll to the group and tell why that particular toy is special to them. Make sure that there is an atmosphere of respect and that no one makes fun of what others say, so that no child is embarrassed or feels bad for opening up to the group and sharing what they feel for their doll. At these ages, some children may still feel that their favorite teddy bear or doll is their best friend, while other older children may have "outgrown" this stage and may see this as too "childish." Teach them to respect and value everyone's opinions.

After everyone has shared why that doll is special, lead them to talk about friendship. Ask them the following questions and let everyone say their answers and opinions out loud as if it were a brainstorming session...

Is a friend special? What makes a good friend special?

Is a friend more valuable than an object? Why or why not?

As we have already said, many children come to consider their toys as their first friends, and that is okay. The idea is to help them mature a bit in the world of relationships: that they can begin to value friendship more than material things, and that they learn to be good friends.

📝 FOUNDATIONS OF THE THEME

The best teacher in the world established and modeled himself after, what many educators have recognized as the ideal vehicle to transmit any knowledge: LOVE.
Héctor Hermosillo *(Pastorea a tu hijo adolescente)*
[Pastor your adolescent child]

It is one thing to build a relationship and another thing to value it. Every child needs to learn how to build relationships wisely, and know what value to place on a friend.

Let the doll or puppet you brought explain to the children:

Did you know...?

- Friendship is like a very, very big house.

- Building a friendship is like building a house.

- When building a house you can add a garden, a patio, lots of plants, , and many other things and it is very important to put up solid walls so that it never falls.

Question for the children: What things should you put in a friendship so that it is firm and solid like a giant house? (Let the children answer.)

Keep talking, using the puppet:

Sometimes things happen that put the walls of a house at risk of collapsing, like when an earthquake hits. Children, what happens when there is an earthquake?

EVERYTHING SHAAAAAKES! (Have them hold hands and pretend to be in an earthquake.)

A friendship sometimes goes through earthquakes. What things can be like an earthquake for a friendship? (Let them answer, and then you complete the list.)

- **Fights.** When two friends have a misunderstanding.

- **Insults.** When you say something that hurts your friend.

- **Jealousy.** When you are not happy about the good things that happen to your friend.

- **Abandonment.** When you abandon your friend, or they abandon you.

And what can we do to avoid earthquakes in friendship?

- Learn to talk before fighting.

- In the face of any offense, know how to forgive and ask for forgiveness.

- Be happy when something good happens to a friend.

- Never abandon our friends.

The doll or puppet keeps talking:

Who has good friends? (Have all the children raise their hands or shout to respond.)

Whoever thinks they have the most friends should laugh!

Whoever thinks they have the most friends should shout!

Whoever thinks they have the most friends should whistle!

And when an EARTHQUAKE comes... (Make everyone hold hands and fake the earthquake.) we already know what to do to take care of our friendship!

📖 FOCUS ON TRUTH

Read this verse from the book of Proverbs with your children:

One who has unreliable friends soon comes to ruin, but there is a friend who sticks closer than a brother.
(Proverbs 18:24)

From this verse we can learn two things:

- There are friendships that lead us to ruin. Bad friendships can do us a lot of damage.

- There are friends who are more faithful than a sibling. There are friends we can always count on, and they are as close as our siblings.

HELP YOUR CHILDREN UNDERSTAND HOW IMPORTANT IT IS TO CHOOSE THEIR FRIENDS WELL.

That's why we must choose our friends well!

Look at this other verse:

Perfume and incense bring joy to the heart, and the pleasantness of a friend springs from their heartfelt advice.
(Proverbs 27:9)

What can we learn from this verse?

- Good friends give us good advice.

- A good friend brings joy to our lives.

Seeing all these points, help your children understand how important it is for a disciple to choose their friends well.

 INTROSPECTION

This week's phrase talks about the best friend that exists: Jesus!

Jesus is the best friend I can have.

Remember that it will not be enough for the children to write down this phrase in their journals, nor for them to learn it by heart. It is necessary that they reflect on what the phrase means so that they can take ownership of it and thus it can transform their lives!

Can you see Jesus as a friend?

How do you know that you can always count on Jesus?

REFLECT ON A CHARACTER

SONIC

A blue-colored hedgehog with great electrical powers and supersonic speed came to Earth from the planet Mobius. Sonic was so fast that he could go unnoticed among humans.

But he had a problem: he was alone. And who can bear a life without friends?

One day, while playing on a baseball field, he was furious that he had no friends and threw a tantrum so loud that it caused a huge blackout throughout the city. For this reason, the evil scientist Robotnik began to persecute him, to take advantage of his powers. Sonic took refuge in the house of Tom, the sheriff of the place, and he helped him escape from Robotnik.

Thus, together, they began a journey that would lead them to become best friends. Tom initially risked his life to protect the friendly blue hedgehog, and

160

Sonic then did the same to save the entire town from Robotnik, which by that time had already gone berserk.

Since then, Sonic has made many great friends!

QUESTIONS FOR YOUR DISCIPLES:

- Have you ever felt lonely like Sonic at the beginning? If so, when?

- Do you have a friend that you can count on in any circumstance?

- Are you the kind of friend who can always be counted on?

DAVID AND JONATHAN

King Saul was very angry with David. Since that boy stopped being a shepherd and became a warrior killing the giant Goliath, he made Saul so jealous that now Saul was chasing him to kill him.

But David was not alone. He had a good friend: Jonathan. That's right, the son of King Saul had become David's best friend. Both had built a friendship so strong that nothing and no one could separate them.

Learning that the king wanted to kill him, David decided to flee from Saul. But he couldn't do it without help. Who do you think helped him?

That's right, his best friend Jonathan. Jonathan knew that his dad was not doing the right thing by going after David. What a difficult situation for Jonathan! He had to decide between telling his father the truth about where David was or helping his friend escape.

Because Jonathan chose the right thing and helped David escape, David soon became king. Jonathan was for sure upset for having to protect his friend from his father, but he make us all see the value of a true friendship.

QUESTIONS FOR YOUR DISCIPLES:

- How do you think David and Jonathan came to have such a trusting relationship?

- Do you have friends like that? Would you like to have them? How do you think you could get them?

 # MOBILIZE

Begin this last section by making sure that all the children copy in their DISCIPLE'S JOURNAL the phrase of the week:

Jesus is the best friend I can have.

If you were using the doll or puppet to lead the meeting until this part, you can continue this section in the same way.

When they have finished copying the phrase, explain that their homework for the week will be to draw a picture of any part they liked from today's lesson. It can be a drawing of one of the puppets or dolls, or it can be about David and Jonathan, about Sonic the hedgehog, or they can even draw the face of a friend they appreciate very much.

After that, when they have the drawing finished and painted, ask your children to teach their parents what they learned about friendship. Remember that the greatest percentage of learning is obtained when we teach in our own words what we have learned!

Tell them that they can also use a puppet or doll at home to tell their families what they were working on during the meeting. This will make it more fun for them! It is not about repeating things from memory to verify that they have learned. Rather, the idea is that they tell what they experienced in class, and through this exercise it will be possible to notice what has really sunken in.

Do not forget to keep in touch with the parents so that they promote the children's work at home in their journals each week. With so much homework and other activities, children may forget it or not give it much importance. They may also be afraid or embarrassed to share what they are learning with their parents. Help them overcome that!

At the end of this class, we encourage you to invite a boy and a girl to pray, and it is not a bad idea to prepare them beforehand. The subject of friendship is very close to them, and you can tell them that one of them can pray that all the children in the class find good friends and that the other can pray that each of them will be good friends.

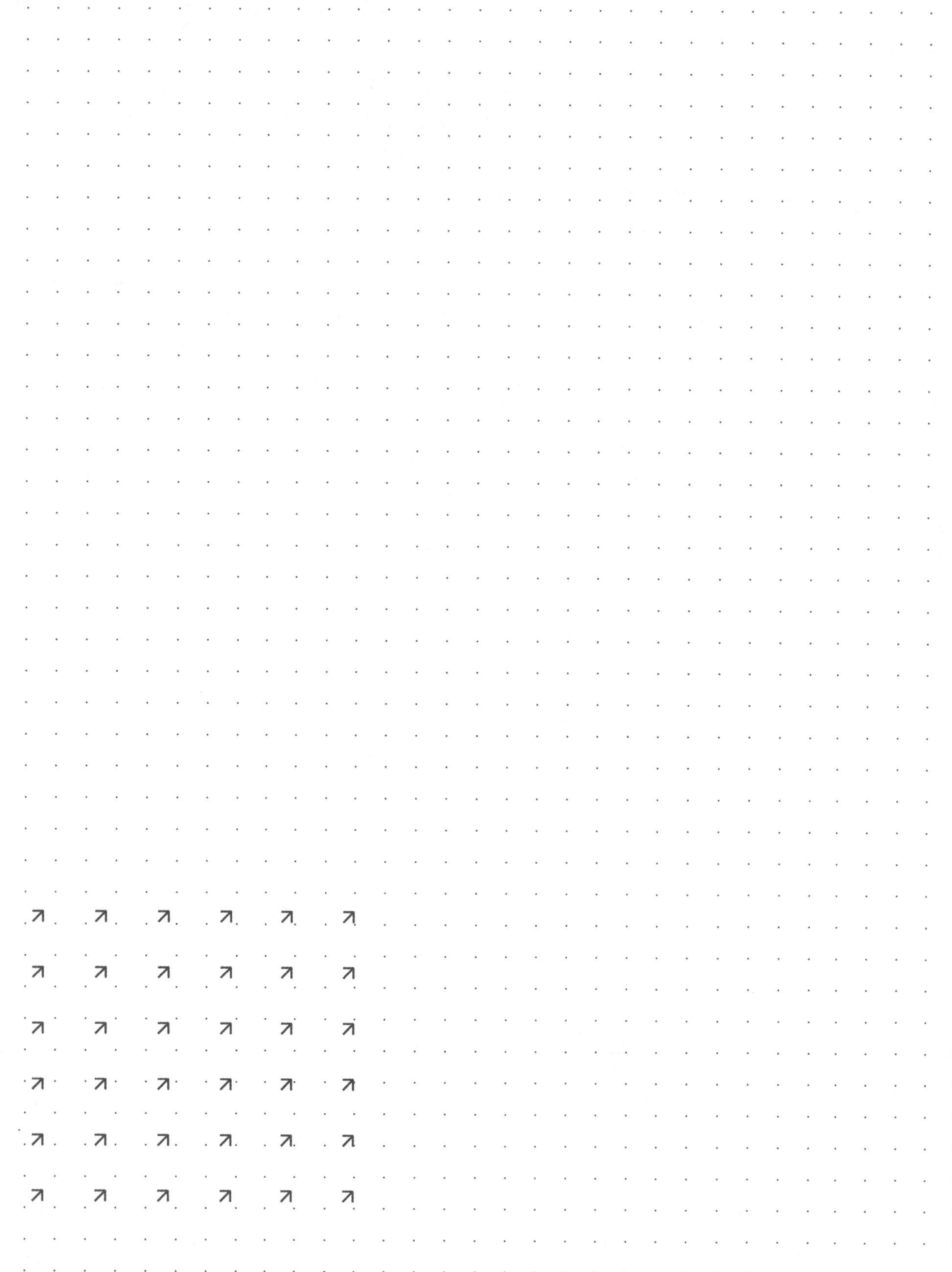

LESSON 9

GOD'S PERFECT DESIGN

*Before the mountains were born or you brought forth the
whole world, from everlasting to everlasting
you are God.*

Psalm 90:2

God makes all things right and everything is good under the sun when we put it to the use God wants us to put it to. Today our boys and girls will not hear that, not even from people who go to a Christian church. We call good bad and bad good and there are a lot of theories and ideologies that change the use and purpose of everything. It is as if someone entered a store at night and changed the labels on everything. That's why it is vital that we teach them that there is nothing more intelligent than doing God's will.

 AVALANCHE OF IDEAS

ACTIVITY: CREATIVITY IN PROGRESS

Materials: Play-Doh, posters, and colored pencils

For today's lesson, you can ask each child to bring a poster, either white or colored, and some Play-Doh of any color. Or, if your ministry has funds for materials, you can purchase them yourself.

What is this activity about?

As a first step, ask each disciple to invent a figure and design it on the poster using the Play-Doh. It can be something of God's creation or something that does not exist, something imaginary. There are no limits on this. The only condition is that the figure has both a part of it that is real and a part of it that is invented by them.

Explain that when everyone has finished, each child should present their creation in front of the group, describing all the features it has. They will be able to talk about its size, whether it is alive or not, how it grows, what it is good for or what use it is if it is an object, etc.

Before they get to work, make sure they get the idea right. Here's an example, but you can give them several similar examples until you feel like everyone understands.

Example:

- My creation is a tree.

- The real part: It provides shade for many animals and is as big as a house.

- The invented part: It's purple and the branches are shaped like birds.

At the end, you can leave the children's creations "on display" in the room and invite the families to see them. (If they have the names of each child written on them it will be better.) Or you can send each child home with their artwork so they can show it to their family.

FOUNDATIONS OF THE THEME

God used his creative power to devise a universe full of wonder and amazing details. The delicacy of the roses and butterflies contrasts with the imposing mountains, and the light of the stars in the sky spills over the rushing rivers and seas to bathe the dry land.

Although many people doubt his existence, God is the creator of everything that exists, and his creation is perfect!

Some myths that we must debunk in the minds of children:

- "Science is contrary to faith." In reality, science does not contradict the Bible, and can even serve as a support to ratify its truths. Let's teach our children that faith and science are not opposites, but complement each other!

LET'S TEACH OUR CHILDREN THAT THE BIBLE IS AS REAL AS SCIENCE!

- "Science is real and the Bible is fantasy." The school system, and in some cases theology itself, has been separating these two things. Let's teach our children that the Bible is as real as science!

- "The things of God and faith can never be explained". Often people think that science is verifiable and that things of faith cannot be explained. Let's teach children that there are things of science and things of faith that can be perfectly explained, just as there are things of both science and faith that cannot be fully explained!

How much damage has been done by the narrative that science was founded against the church! On the contrary! They were people inspired by God who saw that it was reasonable to acquire knowledge through intelligent observation and reading the book of Nature.
Alex Sampedro *(Artesano) [Craftsman]*

Put in the minds of children these new truths with biblical support:

- God created faith and science. God made it all!

- The Bible is real and can be fully verified.

- There are things that neither science nor faith can explain.

Keep in mind that the teaching will stick with the children more if you use different elements to represent what you are saying. For example, you could use a light bulb or a magnifying glass to talk about science, and a cross or a Bible to talk about faith.

But why is the Bible so difficult to understand?

WHEN GOD MAKES SOMETHING, HE MAKES IT PERFECT.

Well, there are portions of the Holy Scriptures that require a little more study to fully understand, and there are others that are more "kid-friendly" to read. What we must achieve is that they are convinced that everything that is written there is real, and that it is not an invention of human beings.

Here are some truths to share with children:

GOD'S CREATION IS A PERFECT DESIGN

When God makes something, he makes it perfect. There is no detail that escapes him.

- God made the world full of science, with physical laws, chemical properties, and universal principles that man has discovered over time.

- God made man with a moral capacity to recognize right and wrong, and to be able to choose to do right.

- Nature works perfectly thanks to the fact that God made everything perfect, although sometimes human beings have taken it upon themselves to damage God's perfection. That is why we must take care of creation!

The biblical writers knew the difference between fiction and fact, and God gave each of them directions as they carefully wrote about their experiences with Him.
Josh McDowell *(Children Demand a Verdict)*

THE DESIGN OF THE HUMAN BEING IS PERFECT

- Science has been able to confirm that the human being is a complex and detailed marvel that works perfectly.

- Many of the inventions that now make our lives easier have been inspired by the functioning of the human body or by nature.

THE LAWS THAT GOVERN THE UNIVERSE WERE PLACED BY GOD

- There are physical laws that govern the natural world.

- There are moral laws that govern the behavior of human beings.

- There are spiritual laws that govern the supernatural dimension.

Another point that children need to understand is that creation cannot be imitated. There is nothing and no one that can replicate what God has done. Human beings can try to reproduce something similar based on what already exists, taking it as a model, but they will never be able to create something from nothing.

Now, if everything is so perfect and special, it is very clear that there must be an intelligent designer behind it, right? Of course! That is our great God!

📖 FOCUS ON TRUTH

To start the next section, a good idea would be to show a video displaying the wonders of God's creation: nature, animals of all species, rivers, and seas.

Another good idea could be that you get a white lab coat and act like a scientist. That will make the kids pay more attention!

Explain to them that there is someone responsible for creation, and that is our God. Read the following verse together:

For every house is built by someone, but God is the builder of everything.

(Hebrews 3:4)

The human being, because we are made in the image of God, is capable of creating through art and science. However, this creation is a transformation of something that already exists.

- A building requires bricks, cement, and other materials that come together to make something different. (Here you can show pictures of how a building is built or bring to class some small pieces of wood and some Play-Doh to put them together, pretending to build something.)

- An artist can take a blank canvas and colored paints, and transform it into a work of art. (Here you can have the necessary elements ready and act as if you were an artist, quickly painting some strokes to illustrate what you are saying.)

But only God is capable of creating out of nothing, just by saying the words!

By the word of the lord the heavens were made, their starry host by the breath of his mouth.
(Psalm 33:6)

Now encourage the group:

- Raise your hand if you can create a painting!

- Now raise your hand if you can invent a story!

- Raise your hand if you can build a sandcastle!

- And now, raise your hand if you can invent something that doesn't exist yet, using materials that don't exist either! (Impossible! Human beings cannot create from nothing. Only God can!)

Next, explain to the children that just as God created nature, he also created the human being.

So God created mankind in his own image, in the image of God he created them; male and female he created them.
(Genesis 1:27)

That is why if you are a disciple of Christ and are faithful to what the Bible says, you will know that there are only those two biological genders: male and female. This is how God made it, and his design is always perfect. Anything outside of that design is simply a deviation from God's for people!

Also, the Bible says that God created us for a purpose:

For we are God's handiwork, created in Christ Jesus to do good works, which God prepared in advance for us to do.
(Ephesians 2:10)

God had a plan for humanity, and it was that we always do good things.

How could we summarize what we have talked about so far?

- God is the creator of everything. He is both a builder and an inventor.

- God made all things by the power of his word.

- He made everything perfect so that it fulfills a purpose.

- The purpose of the human being is to do good works.

- God designed human beings as male and female. Anything that deviates from this is outside of his design.

Many people do not want to live according to God's perfect design, and that is why they invent new ways of living, new criteria about love, and new ways of thinking. But whatever they do, if the things they do are outside of the design that God planned, then they are not good works.

For from him and through him and for him are all things.
Romans 11:36

 # INTROSPECTION

This week's phrase is:

God's plan is perfect.

Help children to reflect with some questions:

- In what things of creation or nature can you notice God's perfect design?

- What things in this world have deviated from God's plan?

- Why were human beings created?

REFLECT ON A CHARACTER

WOODY

Andy loved his childhood toy. Woody was the cowboy that every child would like to have. He had been designed to be a faithful companion. And he could never forget this, since he had his friend's name written on his boot.

Toy Story is one of the most famous movies among children because it brought the world of toys to life. Thanks to Woody and his friends we were able to imagine what happens between the toys when people are not around. This is how toys reached the hearts of children and adults, and *Toy Story* became famous for bringing audiences to tears, including parents.

What made this possible? Design. Woody wasn't just a toy. He had feelings, he was a leader, he showed kindness and patience to everyone. But above all else, Woody was designed to be a faithful friend. He would never leave Andy, because he felt that he had been designed to be with him forever! And although the various adventures he had to go through might have diverted him from this path, Woody never forgot the purpose for which he was created: to be the best companion a child could have.

QUESTIONS FOR YOUR DISCIPLES:

- How do you think Woody would have felt if at a certain point in the movie he had decided to forget the purpose for which he had been created?

- How do you think staying true to his purpose to the end made him feel?

ESTHER

When Esther was called by King Xerxes to be part of the court of maidens from whom he would choose a wife, she knew she had a great purpose. For an entire year she went through all the necessary processes to purify herself so that she could stand before the king, and when that finally happened, Xerxes immediately chose her and made her his queen. Until then Esther had been protected by her cousin Mordecai, and suddenly she went to live in the king's palace!

Hadasa (that was the Hebrew name for Esther) was an intelligent girl, and she knew how to follow Mordecai's advice and keep quiet about her identity and that of her people, otherwise the Persian king could have decided to kill her.

The book of Esther tells us the story of when, due to the machinations of the evil Haman, Mordecai and all the Hebrew people were about to die because of an edict from the king, who had been manipulated by Haman.

Esther acted wisely and managed to save all her people, and not only that, but she also managed to get her cousin Mordecai a privileged position within the empire that King Xerxes ruled.

She knew that she had been born for a great purpose, and that purpose was evidently to save God's people from being annihilated! That had been God's perfect design, and his perfect will was fulfilled in Esther.

QUESTIONS FOR YOUR DISCIPLES:

- What can we learn from the story of Esther?

- In what way can Esther be an example for us?

🖐 MOBILIZE

Have the children copy the key phrase from this lesson in their DISCIPLE'S JOURNAL:

God's plan is perfect.

Give them Romans 12:2 to read and memorize for the week:

Do not conform to the pattern of this world, but be transformed by the renewing of your mind. Then you will be able to test and approve what God's will is—his good, pleasing and perfect will.

This will be the homework for this week:

Each disciple should study about an animal that does something amazing just because of the instinct that God put in it.

For example:

- Bees build hives with an impressive level of precision.

- Ants build incredibly complex anthills.

- Bats don't have eyes, but they have radar that, using sounds, allows them to locate themselves so they don't crash into things and to find their food.

Each child must draw a picture, glue a photograph, or write a paragraph in their DISCIPLE'S JOURNAL about what they investigated.

What do we gain with this activity?

- Children will be able to see real and practical examples of the wonders of God's creation.

- It is a new opportunity for them to work with their parents, researching together.

- Everything they learn will give them arguments to respond to those who disparage the fact that God created all things.

Do not forget to set aside time in the next class so that they can share with the group what they have studied during the week.

End the meeting by praying that your boys and girls yearn to always live within God's plan and design.

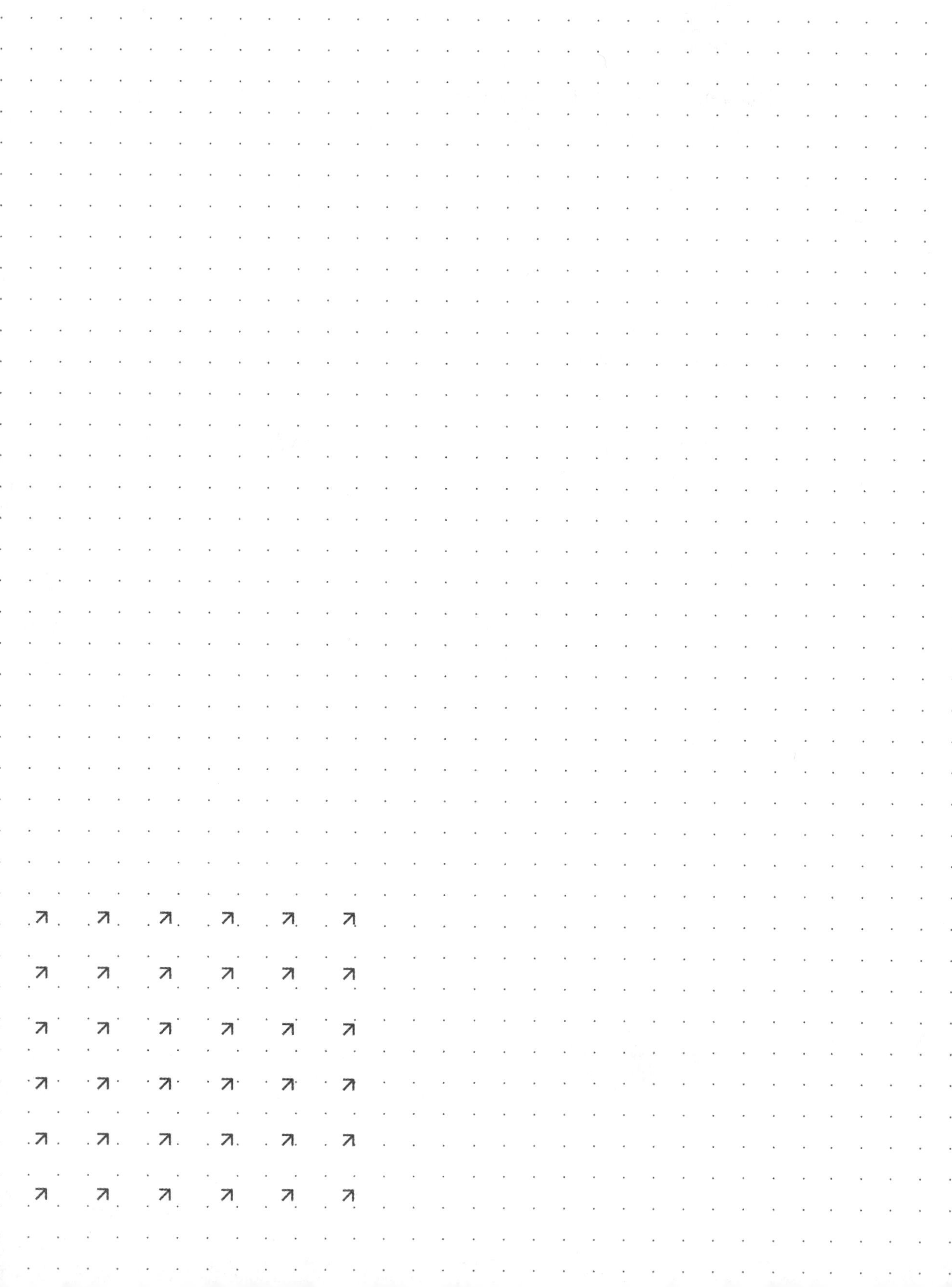

LESSON 10

THE GOOD AND THE BAD

When the Lord makes it clear to you that you must follow Him in this new direction, focus completely on Him and refuse to be distracted by comparisons to others.

Charles R. Swindoll

The end of this book is approaching, but not the end of the Discipleship Project. In this lesson it is vital to lead boys and girls to decide that they will always continue to grow in being like Jesus even when they grow older, and we or their parents are not there with them.

From the beginning of the lessons, we insist that discipleship is a long-term process because the formation of the character of Christ in a disciple is a race that lasts a lifetime. It is a marathon and not a sprint.

This last lesson entitled "The Good and the Bad" aims to lay firm foundations in the boys and girls in your group so that they learn to make their own decisions when adults are not looking at them.

THE FORMATION OF THE CHARACTER OF CHRIST IN A DISCIPLE IS A RACE THAT LASTS A LIFETIME.

We can be sure that they will not be perfect, yet they know how to distinguish right from wrong. They decide to do what is right not to avoid a scolding from their parents or other adults but because they understand that sin is truly bad.

🧠 AVALANCHE OF IDEAS

ACTIVITY: THE ABYSS

Get white masking tape and form a path with it throughout the room where you organize your meetings. They should be two parallel lines of tape separated by the width of one foot or approximately 30 cm. The length will depend on the number of participants you have in your discipleship group.

The game is called "The Abyss." Tell them the following story:

This is a narrow path located high up between two mountains. It is a bridge used to cross from one side to the other. On either side is a deep abyss whose end is unknown, and this is the only known path to reach the other side. They are all stopped on the road, but when they cross the bridge, they find a guard who demands certain conditions that the group must meet in order to pass.

You, as a discipler, must choose those conditions. Here are some examples of what you might request:

- Place yourself in order of height.

- Place by age, or according to the date of birth within the year, starting with those who have a birthday in January.

- Arrange in alphabetical order, by first name.

To achieve the orders that the guard requests, they must agree, help each other, and participate actively. As the game goes on, you must keep reminding them that there is an abyss on either side. If someone crosses the line marked with tape on the floor, they must leave the group, or they will all start over. Give them a few tries so they have fun with the activity, but create the right tensions so that the task isn't too easy for them.

You can choose as many different conditions as you want, but don't spend too much time on it because, like any dynamic activity, it can be tedious if you don't stop on time. The advice is to stop it when you feel it's best and everyone is enjoying it, so they will want to do it again another time.

📝 FOUNDATIONS OF THE THEME

God knew that the human being was at risk of making bad decisions and leaning toward evil. That is why he created various boundaries so that all of us can stay safe within them. It is necessary to learn and exercise self-control to avoid straying from the limits that God has wisely placed in the world!

IT IS NECESSARY TO LEARN TO EXERCISE SELF-CONTROL TO AVOID STRAYING FROM THE LIMITS THAT GOD HAS WISELY PLACED IN THE WORLD!

We need to help them understand that without self-control they will be the best candidates to become slaves to the temptations that come their way. Learning to pause before you react is the key to developing self-control.
Vicki Courtney *(Five conversations you must have with your son)*

Living within the limits that God has set makes us safe, and exceeding those limits puts us at risk.

Help children see that God has set limits for nature:

- The rain does not last forever, because everything would be flooded. The sun is not shining on everyone all the time as it would burn us. The day has a beginning and an end, and then comes the night.

- Some animals can fly, and some cannot. Imagine a cow pooping in the air like a bird. We would have serious problems with cow dung all over our houses and cars!

- Humans cannot fly either. You cannot stop eating for too long. And you can't stay awake forever, because at some point it's time to sleep to restore your strength for the next day.

BOUNDARIES ARE GOOD BECAUSE THEY HELP US DISTINGUISH BETWEEN THE GOOD AND THE BAD SO THAT NOTHING GETS OUT OF CONTROL!

Explain that boundaries are rules that God has intentionally placed to maintain order in all things. In addition to the limits in nature, God has established moral limits, limits in interpersonal relationships, limits in marriages, etc. Every aspect of life has been designed by God to fit into a space where we can all successfully fulfill our purpose without harming others, and still be of benefit to others. Thus, we can differentiate the things that are good and do us good from the things that hurt us or others.

Boundaries are good because they help us distinguish between the good and the bad so that nothing gets out of control!

What happens when the human being crosses the boundaries of God?

- Friendships are lost.

- People get hurt.

- Marriages break up.

- Families are divided.

- People become wicked.

- The rulers turn evil and then come world wars and conflicts.

In fact, a good definition of *sin* is precisely that: crossing the boundaries.

Being clear about the limits that we must embrace as disciples of Jesus gives us enough freedom to live according to God's will, knowing how to distinguish between the good and the bad, and deciding to always do what is good.

What does this have to do with discipleship?

Well, everything!

If we fill ourselves with bad things, this will cause evil to grow in our hearts. If we fill ourselves with good things, we will grow closer in our relationship with Jesus Christ every day.

That's what boundaries are for! They give us a guideline between the good and the bad.

We say that a house is private property because no one can enter it except the owners of that house. If someone enters without permission, that's bad.

No one can enter a house that is not theirs.

No one can enter a country without permission from the police.

No one can touch a person improperly, because there are personal boundaries.

And what happens when someone crosses those boundaries? If you enter a house without permission, you can go to jail.

If you enter a country without authorization, you will be wanted by the police.

If one abuses another in any way, they will be held accountable by law.

Crossing boundaries is not good, because it is living illegally!

📖 FOCUS ON TRUTH

Many people say that God's law is full of prohibitions that make us increasingly unhappy. God did not create laws to put the human being in a prison. On the contrary, he gives the human being the opportunity to see through his eyes the consequences of doing this or that, and he has given us the wisdom to not go further than what he allows.

The book of Genesis describes the day when God gave human beings instructions to live better. Let's tell this story to the children! To do this, you will need to have a few items ready ahead of time:

- Prepare the necessary materials to build two trees with the children.

- Choose what is most useful and easy to get, but try to make it exciting to the children. From drawing and painting the trees on paper attached to the wall, to building them with wood or cardboard. It's up to you!

- You can build the trees any size you want, but keep in mind that the bigger the better. Then they could stay there for a while to decorate the classroom.

If you think all of this is going to take too long, build the trees with your team before the meeting, and have the kids just do the decorating or painting part.

NOTE: If you are doing a virtual meeting, you can place two images on the screen to represent these trees.

Now read together:

The lord God took the man and put him in the Garden of Eden to work it and take care of it. And the lord God commanded the man, "You are free to eat from any tree in the garden; but you must not eat from the tree of the knowledge of good and evil, for when you eat from it you will certainly die.
(Genesis 2:15-17)

Why did God give them this order?

- **So that they would be free.** Adam and Eve could eat the fruit of all the other trees in the garden of Eden. That is called freedom.

- **So that they would know the boundaries of what was good for them.** There was only one tree they could not eat from. That indicated to them that there was a danger, and they should be obedient.

If only they had followed God's instruction, they would never have sinned or known evil!

God warned Adam and Eve with specific instructions that would keep them from evil, but the human being did not want to listen. To respect these limits or not, was their voluntary choice, and they ended up making the wrong one.

Read this other passage and see what God said to his people:

See, I set before you today life and prosperity, death and destruction. For I command you today to love the lord your God, to walk in obedience to him, and to keep his commands, decrees and laws; then you will live and increase, and the lord your God will bless you in the land you are entering to possess.
(Deuteronomy 30:15-16)

What can we learn from this biblical text?

- Deciding between good and evil is in our hands.

- It all depends on whether or not we choose to obey God.

- There is always a blessing behind being obedient to God's instructions.

However, there are always sad consequences for those who choose to go down an evil path. Read the verses that follow:

But if your heart turns away and you are not obedient, and if you are drawn away to bow down to other gods and worship them, I declare to you this day that you will certainly be destroyed. You will not live long in the land you are crossing the Jordan to enter and possess.
(Deuteronomy 30:17-18)

What can we learn from this passage?

- Just as obedience brings blessing, disobedience brings bad consequences.

- Life is related to obedience.

- Death is related to disobedience.

Now, let's get to work!

- Write the word "OBEDIENCE" on the tree of life.

- Write the word "DISOBEDIENCE" on the tree of the knowledge of good and evil.

- Have the children draw good fruit on the tree of life, and bad, rotten, or wormy fruit on the other tree.

Close this section by having the children identify the two trees and choose one of them. For this, tell them:

Children, today you have the same opportunity that Adam and Eve had to choose between good and evil. What will each decide?

Take turns having everyone stand up and say out loud why they would choose the tree of life.

Some ideas may be:

- Because I don't want to hurt anyone.

- Because I don't want my family to be destroyed.

- Because I want to see God's blessings.

- Because I long for God's best for the world.

Every time a child gets up and says their reason for choosing the tree of life, they should go to the place where the tree was built and sit next to it. They will do so until they are all seated around the tree of life, and then the meeting will continue there.

INTROSPECTION

Help the children to reflect on the following phrase:

There is nothing wiser than obeying God.

An idea to guide them is to show them the following list: My degree of obedience:

- I am very obedient to God and his Word.

- I am more or less obedient to God and his Word.

- I am a little disobedient to God and his Word.

- Tell them to circle the one where they think they are.

ASK THEM:

- Would you like to be more obedient to God and his Word? What do you think you could do to achieve this?

REFLECT ON A CHARACTER

Remember to refer to different characters, considering the age of the children If they're too small or you've never heard of them, this won't make sense. In any case, you can show a short video with some images so that everyone knows who the character you are going to talk about is.

FLASH

Barry Allen is an ordinary young man until the explosion of a particle accelerator gives him the ability to be faster than light or sound. From there he begins his adventures facing other humans affected by the same explosion but who have become evil.

This character taken from the comics offers us a good example of what boundaries mean. In his fight against metahumans, Barry Allen makes use of another of his abilities, which is to travel through time. That wasn't his plan, but those trips to the past and future open dimensional portals creating all sorts of rifts and triggering situations that Barry, in his Flash persona, will have to deal with.

It's not his fault, since his intentions were always good, but along the way he made decisions that made everything worse. That is why human beings do not have the capacity to go so fast or to move in time. Those are boundaries set by God, and they are good!

QUESTIONS FOR YOUR DISCIPLES:

- Would you like to have a supernatural power? If so, which one?

- Can you think of how this could negatively affect the world instead of helping?

- In what way would this example serve to demonstrate that crossing boundaries is never good?

DAVID

David's story is one of the most famous and well-known of all time. The Bible describes the most glorious moments and the darkest moments of many characters. But what things can we learn from David about obedience and boundaries?

When he chose to be obedient:

- David managed to defeat the giant Goliath.

- David respected his authorities. When Saul persecuted David because he was jealous of him, David had opportunities to stop him, and even kill him, but he didn't because Saul was king.

When he chose to be disobedient:

- David fell in love with Bathsheba, who was the wife of another man. Because of that weakness, David lied, sinned, became proud and blinded by sin, and even ended up having Bathsheba's husband killed to stay with her.

QUESTIONS FOR YOUR DISCIPLES:

- If you knew that the consequences of an action would be very bad, would you still do it?

- Do you think it is convenient to respect the limits established by God? Why or why not?

- How can we help each other to trust these boundaries and not break them?

MOBILIZE

Whoever wants to be a good disciple of Jesus must learn to make good decisions.

The task for this week will be to write in the DISCIPLE'S JOURNAL a list of good decisions that each one should make to be more obedient to God and thus move away from evil. The disciples, along with their parents, are in charge of putting the lists together. They do not have to be all the same lists. The important thing is that each child can think of at least two or three things that will make them grow in their obedience to God; they can then be accountable to their parents for that. Being accountable to someone is always helpful for our spiritual growth.

Remember to talk with the parents so they are aware of the topic you are working on and have productive conversations with the children throughout the week about these agreements and commitments to obedience.

Before ending the meeting, remember to give them a moment to copy the phrase of the week in their journals:

There is nothing wiser than obeying God.

This is a perfect time to pray for each boy and girl by name, even if it takes a while. The sentences do not have to be long, but it is important to mention each child's name. If there are too many, divide them and have different members of your team help you pray for them. These sentences should mention the names and a positive adjective about each person. Pray beforehand for this prayer and prepare it carefully.

NOTE: You can summon the families of the boys and girls in your group to come to the next meeting and have a small "graduation ceremony." Have each disciple come with their parents and bring snacks to share among all. That will leave a nice memory for them, and they will surely want to enter a new discipleship process as soon as possible. You can give them a fun Disciples Diploma or certificate.

BIBLIOGRAPHY

- **Brown Rich/Shannon Elisa.** *Trabajemos en familia* (We work as a family.) Dallas, Texas. Editorial E625. 2019.

- *Biblioteca práctica para padres y educadores. Pedagogía y Psicología Infantil.* (Practical library for parents and educators. Child Pedagogy and Psychology.) Madrid, España. Editorial Cultural S.A. 1997.

- **Courtney, Vicki.** *5 conversaciones que usted debe tener con su hijo.* (5 Conversations You Should Have With Your Child.) Miami, Florida. Editorial Patmos. 2013.

- **Hart Archivald/Hart Sylvia.** *La invasión digital.* (The digital invasion.) El Paso, Texas. Editorial Mundo Hispano. 2014.

- **Joiner Reggie/Leys, Lucas.** *Los padres que tus hijos necesitan.* (The parents your children need.) E625. Dallas, Texas. Editorial 2017.

- **López Luis/López Sandy.** *Investigaciones Bíblicas del Antiguo Testamento.* (Biblical investigations of the Old Testament.) Dallas, Texas. Editorial E625. 2018.

- **McDowell, Josh/Johnson, Kevin.** *Los niños demandan un veredicto.* (The children demand a verdict.) El Paso, Texas. Editorial Mundo Hispano. 2005.

- **McDowell, Josh.** *La generación desconectada.* (The disconnected generation.) El Paso, Texas. Editorial Mundo Hispano. 2003.

- **Obando, Esteban/Ibarbalz, Jessica/Gómez, Willy.** *Manual de Consejería para el trabajo con niños.* (Counseling Manual for working with children.) Dallas, Texas. Editorial E625. 2018.

- **Sampedro, Alex.** *Artesano.* (Craftsman.) Dallas, Texas. Editorial E625. 2018.

SOME QUESTIONS YOU SHOULD ANSWER:

WHO IS BEHIND THIS BOOK?

Especialidades 625 is a team of pastors and servants from different countries, different denominations, different church sizes and styles, that love Christ and the new generations.

e625.com

WHAT IS E625.COM ABOUT?

Our passion is to help families and churches in Latin America to find good materials and resources for discipleship of the new generations and that is why our website serves parents, pastors, teachers, and leaders in general 365 days a year through www.e625.com with free resources.

ZONA DE CONTENIDO
PREMIUM

WHAT IS PREMIUM SERVICE?

In addition to reflections and free short materials, we have a service of lessons, series, research, online books, and audiovisual resources to facilitate your task. Your church can access this service per congregation with a monthly subscription that allows all the leaders of a local church to download materials to share as a team and make the necessary copies that they find relevant for the different activities of the congregation or their families.

CAN I EQUIP MYSELF WITH YOUR HELP?

It would be a privilege to help you and with that objective we have our events and our possibilities of formal education. Visit www.e625.com/Eventos to find out about our seminars and go www.institutoE625.com to learn about the online courses offered by Instituto E 6.25

DO YOU WANT CONTINUOUS UPDATES?

Register right now for e625.com updates depending on your field of work: Children- Preteens- Teens- Young Adults.

LET'S LEARN TOGETHER!

e625.com   /e625com

Downloads
Subscription
Recursos
gratis
Store
Chat
Magazine
INSTITUTO
e6
25
Online Education
www.institutoe625.com
Books
Seminars
Events
e625.com